growing up gourmet

growing up gourmet

125 Healthy Meals for Everybody and Every Baby

Jennifer Carlson

with Jennifer House, MSc, RD

ATRIA BOOKS

New York   London   Toronto   Sydney   New Delhi

ATRIA BOOKS

An Imprint of Simon & Schuster, Inc.
1230 Avenue of the Americas
New York, NY 10020

First Atria Books hardcover edition June 2016

ATRIA BOOKS and colophon are trademarks of Simon & Schuster, Inc.

For information about special discounts for bulk purchases, please contact Simon & Schuster Special Sales at 1-866-506-1949 or business@simonandschuster.com.

The Simon & Schuster Speakers Bureau can bring authors to your live event. For more information or to book an event contact the Simon & Schuster Speakers Bureau at 1-866-248-3049 or visit our website at www.simonspeakers.com.

Designed by Renata De Oliveira

Manufactured in the United States of America

10 9 8 7 6 5 4 3 2 1

Library of Congress Cataloging-in-Publication Data

Names: Carlson, Jennifer, 1975– author.
Title: Growing up gourmet : 125 healthy meals for everybody and every baby / Jennifer Carlson.
Description: First Atria Books hardcover edition. | New York : Atria Books, [2016]
Identifiers: LCCN 2015046385 (print) | LCCN 2015046951 (ebook) | ISBN 9781501110559 (hardback) | ISBN 9781501110566 (ebook) | ISBN 9781501110566 (eBook)
Subjects: LCSH: Infants—Nutrition. | Toddlers—Nutrition. | Baby foods. | BISAC: COOKING / Baby Food. | COOKING / Specific Ingredients / Natural Foods. | COOKING / Health & Healing / Allergy.
Classification: LCC RJ216 .C33 2016 (print) | LCC RJ216 (ebook) | DDC 641.5/6222—dc23
LC record available at http://lccn.loc.gov/2015046385

ISBN 978-1-9821-5806-4
ISBN 978-1-5011-1056-6 (ebook)

For my talented and loving little
inspirations, Finley and Eamon . . . who
ignited a passion within me that I did
not know was possible. May your love
of good food continue to grow.

contents

introduction

If you are picking up this book, chances are you are a new mom or will soon be a mom. Let me welcome you! You are entering a world full of wonder, for both you and your baby, and you are going to learn much as you explore it together.

I'm sure you've heard of many of the ways in which your life is about to change—the scattered sleep schedules, the end of privacy, the complications of a night out (even to a movie!)—but there are still other changes that are unexpected, revelatory, and highly personal. For me, the biggest surprise came when I realized how fulfilled I felt in coming up with delicious, wholesome, homemade meals for my baby, and for the babies of my friends. One thing led to the next, and before I knew it, I was feeding more babies than I could count through the Baby Gourmet stand at the Calgary Farmers' Market. Today, the recipes I came up with for my own little ones can be found wherever baby foods are sold in Canada, to the same quality standard I held for what I fed to my own Finley and Eamon.

So how exactly did Baby Gourmet come to be? Quite simply, it came from love. When my daughter, Finley, was born ten years ago, the depth of love I felt for her overwhelmed me, and I wanted the best for her in everything. I felt the same way when my son, Eamon, was born a couple years later. You gain in knowledge and experience after your first child, but that surge of hope and love for your new baby is a transformative one, no matter how many times it happens.

And I suppose you could say it began in my own childhood, with my mom. When I became a mother, I started to see my own mother's actions in a clearer light. I understood in a more profound way what my mother felt for my sister and me, and how she showed us that love. My mom had a garden in the backyard and made everything from scratch, even our yogurt. From the very first, my sister Jill and I were raised with meals of the purest ingredients, made right in our home, from our own plants. To this day we both still love a huge variety of foods and spending time outside. We view the earth as both our breadbasket and our playground. I knew that when I had children of my own, I would want them to have the same experience so that from early on they would develop an appreciation for food—real, whole food, where it comes from, and its importance in our lives.

I know what you're thinking: That sounds great, but our days are so busy, how do you find the time to make all of those meals from scratch? Trust me, this journey was not without heartache, mess, and, sometimes, hours of work that yielded nothing but a kitchen full of dirty dishes! But while most people leave the baby food stage behind pretty quickly, I have spent the last ten years obsessed with it, and I promise you there are shortcuts you can take to ensure the highest quality results in the most time-efficient way possible. Remember, gourmet does not have to be challenging—it just has to start with the freshest, most wholesome ingredients available.

When I decided that I would make all of my daughter's baby food, I read everything I could find on the topic—how to introduce foods to babies, the best ways to prepare them for texture, and which foods to introduce when. In terms of nutrition, I relied generally on common sense: The more natural the foods, the better to ensure baby gets the essential vitamins and nutrients baby needs to grow and develop. A well-balanced menu for the day would include proteins, healthy fats, fruits, and vegetables—the same, really, as you should do for yourself.

But the real learning came from old-fashioned trial and error. The trick I found was to develop recipes that work for the entire family, so that the whole day's labor does not go into a single puree that feeds only the smallest member of the household. Once you have adult-friendly meals that complement baby's food development schedule and translate into something baby will take readily and digest easily, you've struck gold.

I was part of a new moms' group at the time I started experimenting with Finley's foods. (If you aren't part of one yet, I'd recommend looking into joining one, as I found it really valuable to be among so many women who were experiencing with their babies the same firsts as Finley and me.)

We would get together with our babies, share stories, and swap tidbits and hints. Whenever it came to feeding time, the other moms would comment on Finley's meals, with some going so far as to say that Finley ate better than most of the adults in the room. It ended up that a few of the moms offered to pay me to make meals for their babies, too.

When I heard these requests, something clicked in me. I believe in my heart of hearts that every child should be exposed to a wide variety of healthy, delicious, homemade meals, so that they can develop a lifelong taste for foods that will form the foundation of a strong adulthood. Watching Finley eat so well with the meals I had made her was a very emotional experience for me; I felt so proud to have set her up with good habits for life. Every baby deserves that, and, frankly, every mother deserves to feel as good as I felt. From those simple requests in my moms' group, I wanted to enable the widest access possible to first foods that were of the quality I would feed to my own child.

It didn't take long for word about Finley's meals to spread among the mothers in our neighborhood, and soon I had so many requests that it became clear my kitchen wasn't going to be big enough—and that I was going to need some help. My sister, Jill, immediately signed on, and we looked to move Baby Gourmet to the farmers' market in Calgary.

The idea to move to the farmers' market came to us in October, and by January, we had been approved for a stand. As someone who shops at the farmers' market anyway, I knew before we even started on market research that this was my ideal location. Lots of moms take their little ones around a farmers' market every weekend, and market culture encourages everything fresh, wholesome, and homemade. Around three hundred vendors had applied for spaces ahead of us, but our application was rushed to the top because the organizers recognized the value of what we were offering, and no one else was doing anything like it.

Jill and I were psyched. This was the opportunity we had hoped for, and we knew it would be a perfect match. The only downside to all this quick progress was that we were given three weeks to set up. Yes, just three weeks. I have to be honest: These were some of the longest, most labor-intensive days of my life. Jill and I laid the wood floors of our stall by hand and we rented a commercial kitchen in a community center for production, as there was no way either of our home kitchens would suffice. We fitted this commercial kitchen with several mini freezers, then hired my mom and some of her other retired friends to work with us, peeling vegetables and helping with prep. They were our "chop-and-chat" group. The days were long, but with my sister, mother, and family friends around, I knew we had something special.

Once we had the stand and the kitchen set up, our weeks took on a manic pace, and we had to follow a strict schedule to make sure everything got done. As we were selling our meals at the market, Jill and I were also shopping there, sourcing all of our ingredients for the coming week's meals from the farmers and growers working around us. We drove the fruits, vegetables, meats, and spices we'd bought over the weekend straight from the market to the kitchen early Monday morning.

Mondays and Tuesdays were dedicated solely to cooking and spooning the purees into ice cube trays, which we would then freeze to create easy meal-by-meal cubes. On Thursdays we would pop out the frozen cubes and package them into little brown paper bags. We then brought all the meals to the market, where Jill and I manned the Baby Gourmet stall on Fridays, Saturdays, and Sundays. Every week of our two years at the farmers' market looked like this, until the volume of demand became too difficult for us to manage on our own.

So Jill and I disbanded the chop-and-chat group, retired the stand, and took a step back to decide how to best expand our production. In business, growth is usually assessed in terms of numbers of people served, but to me, perhaps the most valuable growth we attained through the market related to knowing exactly what moms were looking for when feeding their babies. Over the years I have spoken to thousands of moms whose babies enjoyed our meals, and through their feedback, our recipes have gotten ever better.

To this day, even as Baby Gourmet has become a larger company in order to fulfill the dream of high-quality, organic baby food for all,

Jill and I still "man the stand," so to speak. We are the first two people to see any query or message that comes in. After all, we perfected these meals by talking every week with mothers, hearing their thoughts, finding out what worked for them and what they wanted to see more of. That personal element is key to us, and that firsthand experience over the last decade has made us sure that our recipes are the best available.

I've been thinking about what to include in this book for four years now, since Baby Gourmet started the transition into the larger Canadian market. The reality is that I've been there, I've experienced it all, and within the 125 recipes in this book you'll find the heart and soul of our company, and what has made us the most trusted name in Canadian baby food. Publishing this cookbook furthers my goal of helping as many babies as possible access these well-balanced, wholesome, flavorful meals, and I hope you'll find it helps you reach your goals of healthy, family-friendly home meals, too.

As daunting as it may seem, there are short-cuts and techniques to make it all manageable, whether you're cooking for one baby or a growing family of five. We are looking for the best outcome in the shortest possible time frame, so that you can enjoy time with your loved ones as well.

Remember, too, to be kind to yourself. These months of introducing solids to baby will be full of wide-ranging changes, and as noble as your intentions may be, you have to remain practical about how to carry them out without giving yourself a

nervous breakdown. Nobody is perfect, and there will be moments when it seems nothing works, but the tips I have collected here are meant to save you some time and effort, while not skimping on quality.

If time is simply not on your side and you need absolute convenience, then try one of our Baby Gourmet products. They were developed by Jill and me as the next best thing to homemade and intended to give parents a break from the kitchen with something they can feel good about feeding their baby.

So, are you ready? Let's consider this our own little chop-and-chat session.

chapter 1

introducing your baby to solids:

the adventure begins

Think about how often food plays a part in your favorite memories: the fancy restaurant date nights, the full-tabled holiday feasts, the ripe fruit plucked straight from the tree, warm with sun and heavy with juice. With the switch to solids, this world begins to open to your baby. It's an adventure of taste and texture, from the first basic cereals to the more complex puree blends. It's also a significant time in terms of your child's health. Because this is when your child's palate develops, baby's first foods should not just be tasty but chock-full of high-quality, healthy ingredients. Introducing baby to a wide variety of essential nutrients right from the start forms the foundation of a strong body, mind, and immune system. As a parent, you can best ensure that what goes into your baby's foods meets these standards. Yes, the move to solids is an adventure, and like any other adventure, it can also be a terrifying journey, dotted along the way with potential pitfalls. Trust me, in preparing baby food first for my children and then for the business, I have experienced it all, and I have emerged at the other end to tell you everything will be fine. In this book, I will give you all the tools, tips, tricks, recipes, and information you need to make this time the most joyful, delicious, and satisfying transition possible.The day I fed Finley her first bite, I couldn't wait to see her reaction. As someone who has always loved food and cooking—from the flavors and the smells to the textures and colors, you name it, I am in!—I fed her, watching with great excitement for a sign that my little girl shared this love with me. When her smile spread across her cheeks and her little legs kicked with glee, I headed straight to the supermarket to see what kind of first foods they had on the shelves. I picked out a couple that sounded healthy and headed back to feed them to her, but one crack of that jar of green beans turned me off the project. These were not green beans, not as I (or any adult) would recognize them. This was a gray-green gelatinous glob with a little pool of bean water floating on the surface. I wouldn't eat this, I thought, so why should Finley? That day I heard my calling, loud and clear: I was going to make all of Finley's baby food from scratch. I did my research and read everything I could find on cooking, preparing, and storing baby food, becoming a self-taught baby food expert. Some of my experiments Finley went for, others less so, and through this trial and error process I learned what ingredients worked well together and which textures were most appreciated at each age. As every child is different, the trick is to keep trying new food combinations and new methods of preparing them until you find what works for your baby, then work to cultivate those tastes.

be a role model

There is no one in the world your baby admires more than you. You are the apple of their eye and the love of their life, and everything you do captivates them. This is why it is so important to use this opportunity to be a positive role model for your baby's eating habits. If your family has not adopted healthy eating, baby's move to solids is the perfect opportunity to do so. If baby grows up among a family where fresh, nutritious foods are readily available and eaten at every meal, chances are that those habits will become part of their routines and expectations. This will ensure baby has the best start in life, and everyone in the family will feel better for it. If you are buying the groceries, you are the ultimate nutrition decision maker in the house, and you make the call as to what your children will eat. This doesn't mean you shouldn't indulge from time to time; it just means that you lay the ground rules for what is generally acceptable. Let's say you consider French fries your dinner vegetable, and you feed this to your baby as well. This means that your baby will grow up associating salt and saturated fats with acceptable dinner vegetables and be less open to the taste of steamed broccoli and so will miss out on all the fiber and vitamins that broccoli provides. If you haven't already, use baby as an excuse to bring healthy eating into the home—your whole family will fare better for it.

guide to getting started
EAT REAL, FRESH FOOD

A great way to source the best ingredients for your baby food is to go to your local farmers' market. Even if the closest one is a little bit out of the way, it is worth seeking out for its sheer variety of seasonal, locally grown produce and farm-raised poultry and beef, presented by the people who know best. Learning where your food comes from and meeting the farmers who proudly dedicate their lives to cultivating your food adds to the value of your journey and will ensure that you are giving your baby the most flavorful, nutrient-dense foods. Plus, when produce comes from the farmers' market, it is so fresh and tender it requires little prep to cook; sometimes a gentle steam is all you need. From my babies' early days, I made the weekly trip to the farmers' market a must for our family, and I still do. Every Saturday or Sunday, we head down to stock up for the week, and nine years in, they still enjoy helping me select the foods for our weekly menu. Plus, there's the social element: My kids look forward to saying hello to the Greek Gals over lunch or enjoying a freshly baked chocolate croissant at Yum Bakery. They especially delight in the pie competitions and other taste-testing events. So strap your baby in your favorite carrier and get out to your local market. Talk to your baby as you pick through the produce and show them each of the foods as you go. Watch their eyes light up and little legs kick with excitement as they take in the cornucopia of colors and fall in love with the beauty of fresh food.

BE ALERT FOR ALLERGIES AND SENSITIVITIES

First off, be aware of and understand your family medical history. It is common for allergies to run in families, so if Dad has an allergy—be it to peanuts or even something that seems unrelated to food, like hay fever—chances are that baby could have an allergy, too. Be sure to follow your doctor's instructions on introducing solids, which usually consist of introducing one ingredient at a time. I will discuss allergies and intolerances in greater detail in the section on allergies starting on page 6.

UNDERSTAND YOUR BABY'S NEEDS

Making your baby food at home means that every meal can be customized to address your baby's needs. Keeping an eye on your baby's reactions to foods and elements of those foods can provide important information on how best to cook for your baby. If baby has gas, colic, constipation, low iron, or poor sleep, you can adjust their foods using ingredients with properties that can help remedy those issues. My little Finley was very gassy, and Eamon tended toward constipation, so I tweaked my recipes to include ingredients that

assist with digestion. I will talk more about the healing properties of foods later in the book.

DON'T BE AFRAID TO BE AN ADVENTUROUS COOK

The days of jarred congealed sweet potatoes, peas, and carrots are over! Yes, there are certain foods that will generally be more acceptable at specific stages of food introduction (which I will cover in the next chapter), but don't be afraid to delve into the great wide world of food options. If baby doesn't like peas, prepare some of the other greens, like broccoli, collards, Swiss chard, or kale—you might find one that baby takes to and can't get enough of. And if the texture of cooked and pureed meats isn't working for baby, why not incorporate an alternative source of protein, such as chia, quinoa, lentils, or Greek yogurt? Plant-based proteins are easy on the digestive system and incorporate well into recipes, so give them a try.

Healthy fats such as olive oil, flaxseed oil, and coconut oil should be part of your food prep, and approach herbs and spices with an open mind, as their complex flavors encourage palate development. A pinch of cinnamon, cardamom, sage, or basil can transform a simple puree into an exciting new experience.

As baby's food adventure develops in duration and breadth, you'll be amazed at what they'll be open to trying (and, sometimes, at what they'll refuse). I was shocked to find that Finley loved garlic cream cheese but wouldn't touch cooked egg yolks. Encourage your little ones to find their individual tastes and express their opinions. Trust me, they will let you know if you've gone a little too far with the garlic clove!

DON'T GIVE UP

As with many of life's journeys, there will be times along your baby's path to solid foods when you'll want to wave the white flag. You'll be exhausted, your kitchen will look like a disaster zone (I used to call mine the "baby gour-mess"), and despite all your efforts, baby won't take any of the new foods. You'll be on the verge of chucking the food prep into the trash and indulging in a little "me time."

Trust me, I have been there—it will happen, and it will probably happen again. When it does, here's what you do:

TAKE THE "ME TIME." Make a cup of tea, then step away from the kitchen. Sit down on a comfy chair and take a deep breath. Remind yourself that all of this is for your baby, so that your baby can have the strongest start in life. Know that you are doing your best, and that is all baby needs.

Once you've made it over that hurdle, I have two magic words to make your week run a little more smoothly:

BATCH FREEZE. Having frozen meals ready to thaw and serve will revolutionize your time management and be the answer to your prayers when you're too tired or busy to cook. Sunday is my cooking day, and when I was making food for my babies, I put their purees into ice cube trays so that they would have a ready-made rainbow of fruits, veggies, and proteins on hand for mixing and matching at mealtimes during the week.

That said, here are some common problems you may encounter and how to approach them:

YOU ARE TOO TIRED AND/OR TOO BUSY: This is easy. Just listen to your body. If you need a break, take one. Even if you don't have any frozen meals to serve, the next best thing is a high-quality, prepackaged baby food. Keep a supply of these in your pantry exactly for these occasions. Now, I started a baby food company but I am still the first person to preach the benefits of cooking for baby at home. I also realize this isn't always possible, so we expanded the company so that every parent could take advantage of the next best thing. I built Baby Gourmet knowing how busy parents are and recognizing the need for quick meals they can feel good about.

YOUR KITCHEN IS WRECKED, BUT YOU CAN'T BEAR TO SCRUB ANOTHER POT: Clean little by little, as you go, and dedicate one or two days a week to cooking. (Remember, batch freeze!) This way, you'll have to do the hard work only a couple times a week.

YOU'VE HAD ENOUGH OF THE PEELING, THE CHOPPING, THE DICING: While I emphasize the value of using local, fresh ingredients whenever possible, I also know that this isn't always realistic. Pre-prepped fruits and veggies are easily found in the frozen aisle and will save you lots of time when you need to put together a quick meal. My preference is Stahlbush Island Farms, an eco-sustainable farm in Oregon that produces an impressive variety of organic fruits, veggies, legumes, and grains, all prepared and ready to use straight from your local supermarket freezer aisle. I'll let you in on a secret: I trust Stahlbush so much, we use their produce in our Baby Gourmet products.

YOUR BABY WON'T EAT THE FOOD YOU'VE MADE: Again, this is very common, so don't be surprised when (not if) it happens to you. Statistics say that it can take around ten exposures to a particular flavor before a baby will develop a taste for it. If baby isn't gobbling the greens on the first bite, just keep trying at each sitting, for up to ten attempts. If by that tenth time baby still refuses, then put that broccoli aside for a few months and try later. There are plenty of other nutrient powerhouse foods to try. Another tried-and-true trick is to mix the disliked food with something they find more palatable, probably a bit sweeter—puree the broccoli with apple, pear, or sweet potato and try again, gradually reducing how much of the baby's preferred ingredient you add each time until baby can take the new food on its own.

allergies and intolerances: introducing allergenic foods to baby

Dietitian's note: The following information is based on the 2013 Nutrition for Healthy Term Infants[1] document, created in collaboration with Health Canada, Canadian Pediatric Society, Dietitians of Canada, and the Breastfeeding Committee for Canada. Thanks to recent research on allergies and how they develop, introducing new foods to baby has become a whole lot easier.

In December 2013, the Canadian Pediatric Society and the Canadian Society of Allergy and Clinical Immunology released a joint statement regarding food allergens entitled "Dietary Exposures and Allergy Prevention in High-risk Infants."[2] This statement said that pregnant and nursing mothers do not need to avoid any foods, and that there's no benefit to delaying introduction of even the most allergenic proteins after six months of age—in fact, delaying introduction may increase a baby's risk of developing an allergy. This applies to both low- and high-risk situations (in which a parent or sibling has an allergy), but not to infants with known food allergies.

While previous guidelines have suggested waiting to introduce such potential allergens as nuts, eggs, and seafood until infants are one to three years old, this was not based on evidence, just expert opinion. Newer observational studies show that delaying allergen introduction has actually caused an increase in allergies. In other countries, where children are introduced to peanut products much earlier, there is a much lower rate of peanut allergy.

The newest research results support that early introduction of allergens may actually *prevent* allergy. In the Learning Early About Peanut Allergy (LEAP) study, over 600 children at high risk for peanut allergy were randomized to either consume peanuts regularly starting between the ages of four to eleven months or to avoid peanut protein until age five. The results showed that in the early-introduction group, only 3 percent developed a peanut allergy. The group that avoided peanuts had a 17 percent allergy rate![3]

So the Canadian Pediatric Society's position paper applies to high-risk infants but not to babies who already have known food allergies. But what if your baby has known allergies? This paper discourages allergy testing in young children, as the results are so inaccurate. An allergist can help you decide if an oral food test is a good idea. While it is true that delaying introduction of a food does not prevent, and may in fact increase, the incidence of an allergy, the parents' comfort level also needs to be considered. After all, a three-year-old child can likely tell you if their throat is itchy, while a six-month-old baby cannot.

So I can feed my baby peanuts and nuts at six months? Eggs? Shellfish? Wheat? Yes, please do! While it's still wise to introduce these more allergenic foods a few days apart and watch your baby for any signs of allergy, do introduce them early in your baby's starting-solids career and continue to feed them regularly (at least three times per week) to encourage tolerance.

Now have fun, and bon appétit, baby!

INTRODUCING DAIRY TO BABY

Following the research discussed above, the most recent guidelines on when to introduce allergens to baby suggest that all foods—including dairy—can be introduced at six months. There's no greater risk that your child will develop an allergy if you introduce a food at six months instead of twelve months, and some studies suggest that earlier might be better.

For dairy, I suggest starting your baby on plain, full-fat yogurt. You can mix in a fruit puree for flavor, if you like. Then, if baby is happy with that, you can move on to fluffy piles of grated

gets lots of iron from their diet? Then it's okay to introduce cow's milk regularly at nine months. If your baby doesn't love solids and subsists mostly on breast milk or formula, then wait until they are a full twelve months.

Once your baby is drinking cow's milk regularly, two to three cups per day is the maximum they should consume. Higher intakes can be associated with low iron and anemia. Often toddlers really, really like cow's milk and will drink it all day. Then the parents claim their child is a picky eater, and it's quick to spot the problem: He drinks six cups of milk per day, so of course he isn't hungry for other food! One way to slow down milk intake is to offer it only at meals, in an open cup instead of a sippy cup or bottle. It's so easy for little ones to toddle around all day sipping on milk from the bottle or sippy, which can lead to tooth decay. And remember, as long as you are nursing, your baby won't need cow's milk. No milk is more nutritious than mother's milk, after all!

WHAT'S THE STORY WITH GRAINS?

On message boards and in online communities, it's increasingly common to hear people suggest that it may be better to delay introducing baby to grains until at least year one, maybe even year two. The reason, they say, is that until that age, babies' bodies don't produce enough amylase, an enzyme that digests complex carbohydrates. It sure sounds scientific.

But what about the complex carbs in fruits and veggies? I've never heard any doctor suggest

cheese that your child can pick up on his own, followed by full-fat cow's milk.

That said, it is recommended to wait to give your baby cow's milk as their main milk source until they are nine to twelve months old. This isn't related to allergies but rather to iron levels, because cow's milk is low in iron and can actually inhibit iron absorption.

So when baby has reached nine months, how do you know if baby is ready to incorporate cow's milk as a major part of his or her diet? This depends on how much solid food baby is eating. Do you have a baby who eats plenty of solids and a delay in introducing vegetables, so this theory sounded a bit fishy to me, an offshoot of the anti-grain movement that is currently the (anti-?) toast of the adult world. It struck me as sad, really: Are we transferring our newest fad diet onto our babies?

So with my dietitian, I decided to do some research, and here's what we found: Amylase is present in saliva, as well as produced by the pancreas. To look first at salivary amylase, it's important to keep in mind that very little digestion occurs in the mouth—it's almost all in the small intestine. Normally, salivary amylase is deactivated when it reaches the stomach due to the acidity there.

However, it is true that salivary amylase is responsible for the beginning of carbohydrate breakdown and is found at very low levels in newborns. But is it low until a year or two of age? No. When your baby is between three and six months old, salivary amylase increases in abundance.[4] Another study found it to be two-thirds of adult levels by three months of age.[5]

Now to move on to the small intestine, where most digestion occurs. Here the pancreas excretes amylase to help break down long carbohydrate chains into simple sugars for digestion. Pancreatic amylase levels are only 3 percent of adult levels in newborns and begin to increase at seven to eight months. Pancreatic amylase levels don't reach full adult values until children are between five and eight years old.[6]

So with limited pancreatic amylase, does this mean a baby can't digest carbs? Basically, complex carbohydrates would make it undigested to the large intestine, where they would be fermented by bacteria, causing gas,[7] and then be absorbed by the colon. Not deadly, but certainly uncomfortable!

According to our research, here are a few of the reasons most babies are capable of digesting complex carbohydrates despite having lower levels of pancreatic amylase: Other enzymes in the small intestine break down carbs so that they can be used for energy instead of just producing gas. Isomaltase and glucoamylase are at mature levels in the term fetus.[8] Glucoamylase splits the multiple glucose molecules from complex carbs so they can be absorbed and is particularly important in infants, who have low levels of pancreatic amylase.

Interestingly, it seems that once complex carb–containing food is introduced, the baby's body responds by secreting additional amylase. The same thing happens with protein introduction and trypsin, the enzyme that digests protein,[9] so the body adapts somewhat to what it is fed.

Breast milk contains a type of salivary amylase, too.[10] As we mentioned earlier, normal salivary amylase is inactivated once it reaches the stomach, due to more acidic pH levels. However, the amylase in breast milk does not react this way, and it continues to work in the small intestine on digesting the breast milk.[11] This amylase activity also transfers to solid foods for breastfed babies, making it easier for them to digest carbs. Again—the wonders of breast milk!

All of this leads me to conclude that even without a lot of pancreatic amylase, the bodies of babies under one year of age can still break down and use starches for fuel. Despite the supposed dangers that some claim to be linked to grain intake in young children, review studies show few established negative consequences of high intakes of carbohydrates for children younger than four years. Basically, the only proven consequence is cavities (which are, of course, influenced by oral hygiene), with no evidence for detrimental effects on nutrient dilution, obesity, diabetes, or cognition.[12] So after introducing some meat and vegetables to your baby, a grain containing gluten should follow fairly soon. It certainly doesn't have to be a commercial infant cereal; it can be wheat pasta, cooked barley, or rye bread—whatever you like. Research shows that gluten should be introduced no earlier than four months and no later than seven months of age, as both of these have been linked to an increased risk of celiac disease.[13] This fits with the newer school of thought in allergy prevention, that delayed exposure may actually be detrimental. So you are safe to follow your health authority's guidelines for starting solids with your baby, and don't worry about the unfounded fearmongering out there!

faq regarding allergies and intolerances

WHAT IS A FOOD ALLERGY?

Food allergies result when our immune system mistakes a food protein for a malicious "invader" and launches an attack. Reactions can occur within minutes of exposure, or even up to two days after eating the food. They can be mild (as in a rash or runny or stuffy nose) or more extreme (vomiting or diarrhea). The most serious allergic reaction is anaphylaxis, during which the throat starts to close and there is difficulty breathing. If this happens, call 911 immediately or administer an EpiPen injection and get follow-up medical care.

WHAT ARE THE MOST COMMON FOOD ALLERGENS?

The "Big Eight" food allergens include peanuts, tree nuts (walnuts, almonds, etc.), sesame seeds, eggs, dairy, soy, fish, and wheat. If your child has a food allergy to dairy, soy, or eggs, the good news is that these allergies are often outgrown.

SHOULD I WAIT TO INTRODUCE NUTS? STRAWBERRIES? EGGS?

As recent research suggests, it may be better to introduce more allergenic foods closer to six months to promote tolerance instead of allergy. So after your baby is six months of age, it's fine to introduce any food you want! The only food you should wait until twelve months to introduce is honey, due to risk of botulism.

HOW COMMON ARE FOOD ALLERGIES?

About 6 percent of children younger than three years old are affected by food allergies. Some children will outgrow certain allergies as their immune system matures. Food intolerances may be more common; these are not caused by an immune system reaction but from inadequate digestion that leads to an unwanted buildup of some food material, such as lactose with lactose intolerance.

WHAT CAUSES FOOD ALLERGIES?

We don't know. One popular theory is the "hygiene hypothesis"—effectively, that our society has become too clean for its own good. Modern kids aren't in contact with enough viruses and bacteria due to the cleanliness of our circumstances, so their immune systems are not worked as rigorously as they have been in previous generations. As a result, their systems pick up on harmless proteins and attack them unnecessarily. Another theory backed up by some research suggests that vitamin D-deficient people have more allergies—yet another reason to make sure your child gets vitamin D daily.[14]

HOW DO I DETERMINE IF MY CHILD HAS A FOOD ALLERGY?

If you think your child may be suffering from a food allergy, the best thing to do is to keep a food and symptoms record. If you notice any foods that seem to be linked to reaction, you can take them out of your child's diet (making sure they still have a balanced diet). If symptoms disappear, you can try adding the food in again to see if symptoms reappear, and you may have your answer. Or if you go for a lab test first, you then can do an elimination and challenge diet with the foods that show as positive from the test. The lab tests can show up to 50 percent false positives (they say you have an allergy to a food, when you really don't), so that is why the elimination and challenge diet can still be important.

IS IT POSSIBLE TO PREVENT ALLERGIES?

During breastfeeding and pregnancy, you don't need to avoid potential allergens. You can eat peanuts when you are pregnant, and it will not increase your baby's chance of having an allergy to them. Breastfeeding itself may be protective against food allergies, especially breastfeeding while you are introducing potential allergens such as wheat.

It is now believed that exposure to more allergenic food proteins early on may actually be protective and promote tolerance. So when starting solid foods for your baby, there is no benefit to delaying common food allergens past six months as health professionals used to recommend.

As noted above, making sure your child has adequate vitamin D intake may possibly be linked preventing allergies as well.

WHAT SHOULD I DO IF MY CHILD HAS FOOD ALLERGIES?

If the allergies are serious, carry an EpiPen at all times. And you will need to become an expert food label reader, searching for all the various names for and incarnations of the allergen you are avoiding. A dietitian can help you with this, as well as making sure your child is on a balanced diet, even if it is quite restricted.

If the allergies are not serious, you can always try reintroducing the food after a few months. Rubbing it on baby's cheek or lip first to see if a rash develops on the skin can give you some idea if your child is still allergic to that food.

when to start solids

Because starting baby on solids is such an exciting first, some mothers may be tempted to get into it a bit too quickly. I've heard of women attempting solids with their babies who are less than four months old, justifying the move by saying everything from "My baby's too big" to "My baby's too small for just breast milk." Remember, physical size is not a trustworthy indicator of a baby's readiness for solid food, and there is definitely such a thing as starting too early. While the guidelines have changed over the years, right now it is recommended that solids be introduced at around six months. Until that time, exclusive breastfeeding is ideal, to help protect baby from gastrointestinal and respiratory infections. But age is just one factor to consider. You should also watch your baby for certain developmental signs, as each baby is different and will be ready a little bit earlier or later.

Before attempting to feed your baby solids, check to see whether baby:

- can sit up (with support is fine) and lean forward a bit
- can close her mouth over the spoon
- can pick up foods to put in her mouth

Once your baby can do all of these things, watch for signs that he or she is excited to try food. I remember my babies practically vibrating at the table when they were five months old, they were so intent on joining us in what we were having!

Babies' gestational age can also affect their readiness for solid foods. If your baby was born preterm, he or she may need a few extra weeks to mature before starting solids. (Preterm babies are often low in iron, so you might want to check with your doctor about a supplement if they aren't ready to start solids.) On the other hand, if your baby was born post-term, perhaps he or she will be ready for solids a bit earlier. Let's say your pregnancy went full term, you had good iron levels in pregnancy yourself, and you practiced delayed umbilical cord clamping after the birth—

then your baby's iron levels should be pretty strong. As always, if there is any doubt, check with your baby's doctor.

When first attempting solid foods, watch carefully to make sure your baby can hold food in her mouth and swallow. Although this is a learned skill and might take a few tries, if your baby still has a strong extrusion reflex (the tongue pushes the food back out), you should wait to try again in a few days or weeks.

Once age and development have been taken into account, just be sure that your baby is ready to start solids, and it's not just Mom or Dad forcing it on them.

TEXTURES FOR YOUR BABY

The newest guidelines in Nutrition for Healthy Term Infants state that all food textures—including lumpy, pureed, and even finger foods—are fine to offer a baby from six months, so you officially don't have to wait to introduce table foods anymore.[15] I like combining traditional purees with some finger foods best, as this way babies can get all the nutrition from easy-to-eat purees while still experimenting and learning by feeding themselves some finger foods.

Safe finger foods include:

- Pieces of soft-cooked vegetables and fruits
- Soft, ripe fruits such as bananas or avocados (you can roll these in infant cereal or wheat germ so that they're easier to grasp)
- Beans and legumes

- Finely minced, ground, or mashed cooked meat or poultry or deboned fish
- Scrambled eggs
- Grated cheese
- Bread crusts or toasts
- Many of the same foods the rest of the family eats, as long as they don't contain a lot of added sugar or salt

GAGGING AND CHOKING

When introducing lumpy purees or finger foods to baby, many parents are afraid of choking, especially if their baby has a sensitive gag reflex and makes those awful gagging noises every time they eat. However, it's important to remember that gagging is not the same thing as choking. Gagging is a normal part of learning to eat for many infants. It's not dangerous; it's just bringing up the food for baby to chew some more before it goes back down.

With actual choking, on the other hand, your baby won't be making any noise (so those gagging sounds are actually a good sign), as their air pipe is blocked. If they are choking, babies will not be able to breathe and will start to turn blue. Every parent should know how to perform infant CPR in case this happens. Always watch when your baby is eating and be particularly vigilant of any potential choking hazards, including popcorn, whole peanuts or nuts, seeds, fish with bones, hard candies, gum, full grapes and cherries, and sausages.

Here are some tips to avoid potentially risky situations: Hot dogs are the most common food that causes choking in children. If you choose to feed your little one these mystery meat bags, make sure you cut them into thin slices, the long way, down the middle. Spread nut butters thinly on toast or crackers, as they can build up on the palate or form a seal on the windpipe if given by spoon. Grate hard fruits and veggies like carrots and apples before offering them to baby. Foods with strings like celery and pineapple should be finely chopped. Remove pits from fruit, and cut small round fruits like grapes and cherries. You can also use a mesh feeder bag when introducing risky foods, such as berries, when your baby is starting out on solids.

nutritional requirements
IRON
When selecting what to start feeding your baby, make sure good sources of iron are high on the list.

You may have heard the saying, "Food before one is just for fun." And to a large extent, that's true and takes pressure off parents who have "small eaters." Food is not just for nutrition, and first solids also allow baby to explore different tastes and textures. But from a nutrient perspective, iron is the main mineral that babies need beyond about six months of age. In fact, between the ages of seven and twelve months, babies need 11 milligrams of iron per day—more than an adult male! So why is iron from food so important your baby?

Iron transports oxygen around the body and is crucial for energy and brain development.

For the first six months, most babies rely on the iron stores they've retained from birth, but this depends on a few factors: Delayed cord clamping after delivery can increase the baby's iron status, while premature babies may have low iron and need a supplement. Babies whose mothers have poor iron may be at increased risk for the same. Around six months, the iron stores from before birth run out, and the risk of iron deficiency anemia is high. Anemia can cause delays in both physical and mental development.

If you're worried about your baby's food intake or iron status, be on the lookout for physical signs of iron deficiency: pale skin, low energy, and decreased appetite and growth. Your doctor can do an easy blood test to check your baby's iron levels if you have concerns.

So what are good starter foods that contain iron? Fortified infant cereal is the standard North American starter food, and if you want to go that route, be sure to choose a whole grain version without added ingredients.

An even better option is meat. Even though the recommendation to start with meats and meat alternatives is fairly standard now, it still seems to shock parents: "Meat?! Isn't it hard for babies to digest meat?"

No. In fact, it is harder for babies to digest grains. Think of the adults in your life. You likely know someone who is intolerant of grains—celiac disease occurs in one in a hundred people—yet how many people do you know who are allergic to meat?

Plus, your baby's body absorbs the iron in meat better than the iron in fortified cereals or other foods. Meat contains heme iron, and depending on whether your blood is low or high in iron, your body will absorb 15 to 35 percent of heme iron consumed. Vegetables, beans, and fortified foods like infant cereals contain nonheme iron. Between 2 and 20 percent of nonheme iron is absorbed, and this absorption can be decreased by other dietary factors like high calcium intake, tannins in tea, and phytates in whole grains and beans. That said, vitamin C can increase absorption of nonheme iron, so if you're going to serve that fortified cereal, make sure you do so with a side of fruit.

A good rule of thumb is that darker meat (like that found in chicken thighs) contains more iron than white meat. Bison and beef are two good starter proteins that are especially high in iron, and you can also include beans, lentils, egg yolk, tofu, edamame, hummus, and cooked spinach for an extra iron boost.

Try to offer a source of iron with each meal, and avoid introducing cow's or goat's milk on a regular basis until you're confident your baby is taking in enough iron from food.

FAT

Babies need fat for brain development and growth. In fact, it is so important for babies that 30 to 40 percent of the calories your baby consumes should come from fat. While you may be used to eating a lower-fat diet, be liberal when adding fat to your baby's meals. Full-fat dairy, avocados, nut butters, olive oil, and coconut oil are all good sources.

VITAMIN D

Vitamin D goes along with calcium in helping bone formation. Vitamin D may also aid in preventing autoimmune disorders, some cancers, and more. Unfortunately, this fat-soluble vitamin occurs naturally in very few foods; our bodies produce vitamin D when the skin is exposed to sun. In the winter, all people living in cold, dark climes should be taking a vitamin D supplement. For infants aged one to three years, the vitamin D recommended dietary allowance is 600 IU per day. And when do you stop giving vitamin D to your baby? Never! You're going to send that kid off to college with supplements.

PROTEIN

Infants have the highest protein requirement per weight compared to any other age group. Proteins form cells and hormones and function as enzymes. It's no exaggeration: Proteins are the building blocks of life.

The recommended dietary allowance for babies aged seven to twelve months is 1.2 grams of protein per kilogram of body weight daily. This is an average of 11 grams of protein per day. For children aged one to three years, the requirement is about 13 grams per day, and for ages four to eight, it is 19 grams per day. Older children aged nine to thirteen years need approximately 34 grams of protein per day. (As a reference, a cup of cow's milk contains 8 grams of protein, while one egg has 6 grams.)

CALCIUM

Build those bones big and strong! Calcium requirements are 700 milligrams a day for infants aged one to three, and they increase to 1000 milligrams per day when a child turns four. One dairy or dairy alternative serving contains about 300 milligrams.

Other good sources of calcium include leafy greens like spinach and kale, beans, and almonds.

VITAMIN C

Vitamin C acts as an antioxidant, picking up free radicals in our bodies. It's also needed for iron absorption and the making of collagen and connective tissues. Children aged seven to twelve months require 50 milligrams per day, ages one to three years need 15 milligrams per day, ages four to eight should get 25 milligrams per day, and ages nine to thirteen, 45 milligrams per day. Fruits and vegetables like citrus fruits, berries, broccoli, and bell peppers are loaded with vitamin C.

VITAMIN A

Vitamin A is necessary for good vision and immune function. For children aged seven to twelve months, the recommended dietary allowance is 500 micrograms per day, for ages one to three it is 300 micrograms, ages four to eight is 400 micrograms, and ages nine to thirteen is 600 micrograms. Preformed vitamin A, or retinol, is found in animal foods like liver, dairy products, and fish. Carotenoids (like beta-carotene) are converted into vitamin A in the body and found mostly in green and orange fruits and vegetables such as broccoli, carrots, spinach, and squash.

FOLATE

The body relies on the B vitamin folate for healthy function at all stages of life, from the formation of a fetus's spine to memory function in older adults. Recommended daily intake for ages seven to twelve months is 80 micrograms per day, ages one to three is 150 micrograms per day, ages four to eight is 200 micrograms per day, and ages nine to thirteen is 300 micrograms per day. Grain products are fortified with folic acid (the synthetic form of folate). Dark green vegetables, beans, and legumes are good food sources of folate.

OMEGA-3 FATTY ACIDS

Omega-3 fats, specifically DHA and EPA, are required for brain development in infants and children. These essential fats cannot be made in our bodies, so we have to get them through our diet. When consumed, omega-3s have anti-inflammatory properties that may also reduce the risk of chronic conditions such as heart disease

Sources of DHA and EPA include fatty fish or algae supplements. Sources of alpha-linolenic acid, another omega-3 (some of which is converted into DHA and EPA in our bodies), include flax, hemp and chia seeds, canola oil, and soybeans. Recommended daily intakes for ages seven to twelve months is 500 milligrams, ages one to three years is 700 milligrams, ages four to eight is 900 milligrams, and ages nine to thirteen is 1200 milligrams (or 1.2 grams).

CARBOHYDRATES

Carbohydrates (commonly known as sugar and starches) provide energy to the cells in the body. Requirements are based on the minimum amount of glucose used by the brain. Children aged seven to twelve months require at least 95 grams per day. After year one, they need a minimum of 130 grams per day. Most carbohydrates occur as starches (which are actually chains of simple sugars strung together) in food. Grain products, like pasta and rice, and some vegetables, like potatoes and corn, contain starches.

ZINC

Zinc helps wounds heal and strengthens immunity. Requirements for ages seven to twelve months are 3 milligrams per day, ages one to three years 3 milligrams per day, ages four to eight years 5 milligrams per day, and ages nine to thirteen 8 milligrams per day. Zinc is found in seafood, meat, lentils, and beans.

PROBIOTICS

Only recently has research begun to explore the microbiodome of the human gut and the integral role gut bacteria play in maintaining health. There are many strains of healthy probiotics found in drop, powder, and capsule form, each used for different health needs. If your baby is on antibiotics, you should definitely consider a probiotic to boost baby's healthy gut bacteria in the face of the antibiotic onslaught. Probiotics may contribute to improved digestion, a lesser risk of eczema and allergies, and decreased bloating, gas, diarrhea, constipation, and colic.

FEEDING A VEGETARIAN BABY

Vegetarian households will have to do a little more work to make sure that baby receives a good balance of foods from all four food groups. From the meat and meat alternatives group, you can include:

- Cooked beans, split peas, lentils
- Tofu
- Vegetarian "meats"
- Nut or seed butters (peanut, almond, sesame seed, pumpkin seed) spread thinly on crackers, toast, or bread, as large globs can cause choking
- Eggs

Protein, zinc, and vitamin B_{12} are nutrients found in meat products that will be especially important for vegetarian babies. Your baby's diet will still be adequate in these nutrients if you include eggs and dairy products in your family's meals. Also make sure baby is getting enough iron and omega-3 fatty acids.

Omega-3 fats are helpful in preventing heart disease and important for eye, nerve, and brain development. Vegetarian sources of omega-3 fats include:

- Oils like canola, flaxseed, walnut, and soybean
- Ground flaxseed
- Soybeans, tofu, and walnuts

However, these foods do not contain DHA, a specific type of omega-3 fat found in fish that is particularly important for baby's eye and brain development. Even if you don't eat fish yourself, consider offering your baby healthy fish like salmon or providing a fish oil supplement for children.
Iron helps carry oxygen to different parts of the body. Iron can be better absorbed by including vitamin C-rich foods like citrus fruits and juices, kiwis, mangoes, melons, potatoes, sweet peppers, broccoli, and some green leafy vegetables with meals. Good vegetarian sources of iron include:

- Soy and soy products like firm or extra firm tofu and fortified soy drinks (for children over two years of age)
- Meat alternatives like textured vegetable protein (TVP) and veggie burgers
- Dried beans like kidney, pinto, and adzuki beans; chickpeas and black-eyed peas; and red, brown, and green lentils
- Fortified grain products
- Nuts and seeds like almonds and sesame seeds
- Fruits like prunes, raisins, and apricots

- Dark green vegetables like collards, okra, and bok choy
- Blackstrap molasses

SPECIAL NOTE FOR VEGAN BABIES

If you are vegan and choose to raise your baby vegan as well, it is strongly encouraged that you breastfeed your baby for the first two years. The other alternative is to offer your baby fortified soy formula until they are two years of age. Other milk alternatives are too low in protein and fat, but beyond age two you can introduce fortified milk alternatives such as soy, almond, hemp, or coconut milk.

To ensure that your baby gets DHA omega-3 fats, you can take an algae oil supplement as a breastfeeding vegan mom. Other sources to offer baby when they are starting solids include sea vegetables or foods fortified with DHA.

Vitamin B_{12} is found only in animal foods and is needed for your baby to thrive and make red blood cells. The recommended daily intake of vitamin B_{12} for babies six to twelve months is .04 micrograms and, for one to three years, 0.9 micrograms. A popular vegan source of vitamin B_{12} is nutritional yeast, which contains 7.9 micrograms per 1.5 tablespoons. Baby would need only ½ to 1 teaspoon per day to meet this daily requirement. Nutritional yeast is inactive yeast full of key nutrients including B vitamins, zinc, and protein. It has a cheesy flavor and works well sprinkled into most savory meals. I like to use it in the same way

I use Parmesan cheese. If you are a breastfeeding mom, make sure to get adequate B_{12} in your diet through fortified foods, supplements, or nutritional yeast; otherwise your milk may be deficient for your baby.

faq on introducing solids

WHAT IS THE FEEDING RELATIONSHIP?

When I started doing research into how to feed my baby, I came upon the work of social worker and dietitian Ellyn Satter and found it invaluable. Satter described important concepts for creating a healthy feeding relationship between parents and their children and a healthy lifetime relationship with food for your child. This "Feeding

Relationship" assigns different responsibilities to the parents and the children.[16]

The parents' Feeding Responsibilities include when the children eat, where they eat, and what they are offered to eat.

- **WHEN:** By year one, your child should be offered three regular meals in addition to two or three snacks daily. The snacks should not be constant nibbles throughout the day, or the baby will not build up an appetite for the next meal.

- **WHERE:** All family members, including babies and toddlers, benefit from eating at the table with the family. It is dangerous for your little one to be eating while running around, and the shared family mealtime helps create a child who is happier and more successful than those who don't share meals at home.

- **WHAT:** The ideal meal includes something from each food group: grains, fruits/vegetables, dairy/dairy alternative, and meat/meat alternative. A great snack would include at least two of the four food groups. The baby can be offered what the rest of the family is eating, provided it is age-appropriate.

Baby's Feeding Responsibilities include how much they want to eat, and if they want to eat at all. When it comes to eating, babies should always take the lead. Let them play with the food you've offered, and if they are finished (which they'll let you know by closing their mouths, turning away, or throwing food), do not try to force them to eat more. Many parents are concerned that their child is not eating enough, but babies are good at regulating their appetites and will not starve themselves. They may eat a lot one day, then almost nothing the next. That is completely normal. When you approach your child's eating habits with a more relaxed attitude, you help your child develop a healthy relationship with food and their appetites that will carry them through life.

If your baby does not eat anything offered at a meal or snack, or even for a day or two, trust that your baby is doing what their body is requesting. If the baby refuses a new food, try not to worry—try again later, perhaps offering the new food with a familiar one so they have something to eat either way. Then you can attempt the new food a few days later, then again, and again! If you have concerns about picky eating, see the section on picky eaters below.

BABY-LED WEANING: WHAT IS IT? SHOULD I DO IT? HOW?

"Weaning" refers to the process of introducing solid foods to your baby. "Baby-led weaning" is the term given to the practice of skipping the purees altogether and going straight to "real" finger foods that baby feeds him- or herself.

I find the term "baby-led weaning" to be misleading, as I think all methods of introducing solids can (and should!) be baby-led. Even if you are feeding your baby pureed food from a spoon, you should always follow their lead, watching them for signs of hunger and fullness and letting them guide the amount they want to eat.

Babies should be enjoying finger foods as soon as they are ready, and if that's at six months, great! Better to see a baby experiment with finger foods than to have a toddler who refuses texture and exists solely on purees.

However, there are benefits to offering purees first. A lot of parents are worried about choking, and of course there is a bigger risk when you're working with solid finger foods. Purees give your baby the chance to learn how to chew and swallow, progressing gently as you add in texture. And it is much easier to ensure your baby is getting good sources of iron when you can offer them pureed meats or fortified infant cereals.

Here are a few tips for those who want to incorporate baby-led weaning. And remember, you can blend these methods of integrating solids so that you offer the pureed meats for iron and then some chopped fruits or veggies and grains as finger foods.

- **CHOKING:** Obviously, stay with your baby while they eat, so you can monitor them. Don't offer round items that baby might choke on, but note that gagging is not the same thing as choking—it's a normal part of learning how to eat—and remember, if they are choking, they will not be making any noise! Also, refrain from putting solid foods into your baby's mouth, as this can be dangerous.

- **ALLERGIES:** As you most often feed baby what you are eating, they may be getting mixed meals right away. You may need to be a bit of a detective if you think your child has an allergy to a new food, and you've offered multiple new foods in one day. But the risk of food allergy in most babies is low, and the newest recommendation is not to delay introducing any allergenic foods. If your baby is higher risk, you may want to wait to introduce mixed meals until your baby has tried the most allergenic foods individually.

- **AMOUNT:** Baby takes the lead as to the amount that he or she will eat at any given time. Don't worry if it's not much; breast milk or formula will still be their main source of nutrition. Don't "top up" with purees because you think your baby hasn't eaten enough, unless you get the sense that baby is frustrated trying to feed and really is hungry. They know their appetite best and will eat as appropriate.

If you're looking to integrate baby-led weaning into your routine, here are some suggestions for first foods:

- Thawed frozen vegetables (like peas, corn, carrots)
- Pieces of banana or other fruits that are either large enough to grip and bite or small enough to pick up with more advanced fingers and not choke
- Beans and legumes
- Chopped cooked eggs
- Pieces of fish
- Slow-cooked meats that are very tender, like ground meat and cut-up meatballs, provide

great sources of iron. You can even let baby chew on a tender pork rib!
- Coat slippery foods like bananas and avocados in infant cereal or wheat germ to make them easier to handle.
- Foods like applesauce, yogurt, and oatmeal can be offered with a spoon.

A main premise (and one of the big benefits) of baby-led weaning is that you feed the baby at family meals, so you don't have to go to the effort of making separate "baby food"—a win for all involved!

WHEN IS THE BEST TIME OF DAY TO INTRODUCE SOLIDS?

Morning is a good time to introduce solids, as babies tend to be hungry at this time, and you will have the rest of the day to watch for a possible allergic reaction.

WHEN STARTING SOLIDS, DO I FEED MY BABY BEFORE OR AFTER A REGULAR MILK FEEDING?

The best time to offer solids is between milk feedings or after a partial milk feeding. That way your baby will still have some appetite to try the solid food, but they won't be starving and get frustrated by their inability to get the food in fast enough to satiate their hunger.

HOW MUCH DO I FEED MY BABY?

When you are just starting with solids, one meal a day is enough. Start with breakfast, as that is when your baby is likely to be hungriest. It also gives baby the full day to work the new foods through their system, rather than starting with dinner and putting them to bed with an upset tummy.

By seven months, your baby can take two meals a day, and by nine months, you can move up to three regular meals per day. By a year, your baby will be eating family foods in a regular adult eating pattern: three meals and a few snacks. As for the amount of food, that is up to baby! Start with a small amount (1 tablespoon) of food, so you don't waste too much if he or she isn't interested. If they are still eager once they are finished, then offer them more until they let you know they are done!

CAN BABY EAT AT THE SAME TIME AS THE ADULTS?

Yes. In fact, you should start family mealtimes as soon as possible. When your baby is first starting solids, have them eat breakfast with you. As they progress through adding more meals and snacks in their first year, they will end up on the same eating schedule as the adults in the family. Sitting and eating with your child takes all of the pressure off of them (as you are eating your own food, not concentrating solely on baby's eating). Family mealtimes also provide the best opportunity for baby to watch and learn from your own healthy eating habits.

WHAT IF MY BABY DOESN'T WANT TO EAT?

It's not uncommon for babies to prefer breast-feeding to eating solids. If your little one isn't interested in solids when you start feeding them, that's okay. Just follow their guidance and don't force or trick them into eating (that means no distracting them with toys or playing "airplane" with the spoon). Just try again tomorrow!

Another thing to try is going straight to baby-friendly finger foods. Some babies are not interested in purees and just want to have what Mom and Dad are eating. Puffed cereal, grated apple or pear, black beans, a strip of avocado, banana, and toast are good starter finger foods. If your baby still doesn't take to solids after about a month of gentle trying, pay attention to signs of potential iron deficiency, like pale skin, fatigue, decreased appetite, and slow growth. Take your baby to the doctor to be tested if you have any doubts.

WHAT IF MY BABY JUST KEEPS EATING AND EATING?

Just keep on feeding them until they give you signs that they are full. These are usually pretty obvious: spitting, closing mouth, turning face, throwing the food, crying, or fussing. If baby appears eager and hungry, it's important to practice responsive feeding and follow his or her cues. If you limit your baby, you may run into issues with binge eating later on—your child will eat as much as they can whenever they get the chance, as they know that parents will restrict their meals. I know it sounds counterintuitive, but limiting food at these early stages can lead to weight problems later in life. Your baby or child knows their own appetite best, so as long as you're providing nutritious, natural food, let them eat the amount they choose.

HOW CAN I PREVENT A PICKY EATER?

From the first solids, the most important thing you can do is to offer your baby lots of different foods, flavors, and textures. Limit highly sweetened or salty foods so that your baby develops a taste for healthy, naturally delicious foods.

Remember to follow responsive feeding with your baby. Feed them the amount they want—whether you think it's too much or too little doesn't matter.

As your baby gets older, you may find that even the easiest baby can turn into a fussy eater. Feeding struggles are common between parents and children of all ages. It is understandable that as a parent, you are concerned if your baby or toddler refuses to eat multiple meals in a row or never wants to try a new food. As a parent, you act as an important role model for your child when it comes to eating. It is important to enjoy healthy foods with your children and encourage positive eating habits for life. But attempting to exert too much control, such as forcing your child to eat, can negatively affect their eating practices. It can lead to your child having an unhealthy relationship with food, not listening to hunger and satiety signals, and potentially experiencing weight issues as an adult. Stop trying to control how much your child eats. No more minimum bites rules. When we force or strongly encourage our child to eat more, the only habit that is reinforced is the power struggle. The child may actually end up eating less than if given the option to choose how much they are hungry for, and mealtime will not be enjoyable for anybody!

Do not provide backup foods if your child refuses what is offered. Not only is it more work

for you, but it also discourages your child from trying new foods when they know they can get what they want.

Do not bribe or reward with dessert and sweets. This puts processed sugar on a pedestal and sets your child up to have a sweet tooth for life. It also tells your child that whatever you have prepared for them to eat is undesirable and must be forced down.

Continue to offer previously refused foods whenever you eat them, with no pressure for your child to join you. And experiment with different forms or preparations. Maybe if they see those sweet potatoes looking more like a fry than a puree, they'll be curious to give them a taste.

Be a good role model. Offer mostly nutritious foods and eat them yourself.

Get your child involved in growing the food, shopping, cooking the meal, and setting the table. They are more likely to eat foods they have played a part in preparing.

HOW DO I GET KIDS TO EAT VEGETABLES?

Countless parents feel the need to win a face-off over vegetables and make kids eat them. If you have fought to force your kids to eat a certain food, you have learned the hard way: Nobody wins that battle. It can prove a major stressor on a family. Mealtimes should be peaceful and replenishing instead of dreaded by everyone. Over the course of a week, most kids who are offered a variety of foods will get the nutrients they need. Don't worry about each individual meal.

SO WHAT DO YOU SUGGEST INSTEAD, IF MY CHILD DOESN'T LIKE VEGGIES?

1. **DON'T FREAK OUT, BUT DON'T GIVE UP:** The most important thing you can do is to offer vegetables repeatedly at regular meals and snack times, without any pressure to eat them. Eventually your child will eat the veggies he or she wants, and over the long run, he or she will eat more veggies and cultivate a lifelong taste for them, rather than a lifelong hatred if he or she is forced to eat them. Follow Ellyn Satter's Division of Responsibility in Feeding and allow your child to choose "if" and "how much" they will eat of the food you have offered them.

2. **INVOLVE YOUR CHILD:** Grow a garden (or even a windowsill pot) of vegetables and herbs. Visit the farmers' market together and ask a farmer about how they grow their carrots. Have your child pick out a new vegetable to try at the grocery store or wash the lettuce for the salad. Getting kids involved in the process will encourage them to taste the food.

3. **TRY DIFFERENT COOKING METHODS:** Kale chips. Zucchini in "fry" form. Veggies raw or overcooked.

4. **OFFER THE FOOD WHEN YOUR CHILD IS HUNGRIEST:** If they are school-age, after school and before dinner is often a time when children are hungry and will eat anything in sight—including the leftover veggies from their lunches!

5. **GIVE VEGETABLES PLAYFUL NICKNAMES:** Kids may eat more "super-sight" carrots than plain old carrots.

6. **TRY DIPS OR SAUCES:** Hummus and yogurt dips provide extra nutrients. I'm not opposed to ranch dressing or ketchup either, provided your child eats the veggies along with them! Cheese sauce on cooked veggies also enhances their flavor.

7. **BE A GOOD ROLE MODEL:** I have a lot of clients who tell me, "My husband won't eat veggies." If that's the case, then why would the children think they should eat veggies? Expand your palate. Someone is watching you!

CAN I SEASON BABY'S FOODS WITH SPICES LIKE CINNAMON AND PAPRIKA?

Yes, please do! Offering a variety of tastes and seasonings just as your baby is starting solids can possibly help reduce picky eating down the road. Flavors such as garlic, ginger, oregano, cinnamon, and nutmeg are fine—just avoid added sugars, salt, colorings, and preservatives.

IS MY CHILD EATING ENOUGH?

I hear from many moms who are stressed out from a recent visit to the doctor or health nurse and worried that their baby, toddler, or child is not eating enough. Genetics and your child's growth patterns are good indicators of their health. The fiftieth percentile on growth charts is not the weight goal for your child. Half of children weigh more, and half weigh less. Some are off the charts in one direction or the other, and if this is their pattern of growth, that is okay.

Or maybe you've seen handouts suggesting a sample or average day's worth of food for babies or children of different ages. This information is just a guideline as to what you can offer your child in a day, and whether or not they choose to eat it is not your concern. Yes, you are the parent, and it's your job to be worried about your baby, but it's not your job to force them to eat a certain amount of solids. As long as baby is happy and active, baby is likely getting enough food.

Try to relax, and know there is not a certain amount of food your baby "should" eat in a day, other than the amount that your baby chooses to eat that particular day—which may be a little, a lot, or nothing at all.

IS MY CHILD EATING TOO MUCH?

If you have been restricting the amount of food that your child is allowed to eat at scheduled meals and snack times, it is possible that they have reacted by overeating when they get the chance. If your child knows that they will not be allowed to eat until they are satisfied, they will compensate by stuffing themselves when they can. However, if you have offered your child multiple portions and not tried to control the amount of food they eat, then they probably really are still hungry.

Children are the best regulators of their own appetite. As parents, we know there are some days (or weeks) that they will eat next to nothing, and we wonder how they survive. Other days, they might do nothing but eat. Their appetite depends on a number of factors: their growth rates, teething, illness, etc. Remember the Feeding Relationship rules: The only role of the child is to determine how much or if they eat what they are offered. If you are worried because your child is overweight, try to remember that people come in all shapes, and weight is not always the best indicator of health.

If you offer your child mostly healthy foods at regular times, in the portions they choose, they will get the food and nutrition they need to reach their healthy weight (which will change as they grow).

DOES MY CHILD NEED SUPPLEMENTS?

For most young children, food intake tends to balance out over time. Each day will likely not contain perfectly allocated amounts of grains, protein, dairy, fruit, and vegetables, but over the span of a week, if your child is offered these healthy foods on a daily basis, their food intake should average out to meet their needs.

As for multivitamins, if your child is a pickier eater, then they can't hurt. Think of them as providing a bit of nutritional insurance, although they can't make up for an unbalanced diet. Children's multivitamins contain small doses of a variety of vitamins and minerals, so they are not harmful and may be beneficial for your child. Most kids don't really need them, but if it makes you feel better to know your child is taking a multivitamin, go ahead.

If your family does not eat fish twice a week, I would recommend a fish oil supplement. Be wary of products labeled simply "omega-3," as these may contain more ALA (from flax, canola, or other sources), rather than the DHA omega-3 type of fat that is most important for development.

And as I mentioned earlier, during winter I would recommend the whole family take a vitamin D supplement. From October through March, our bodies cannot make enough vitamin D from skin exposure to sunlight. If you are especially vigilant about sunscreen in sunnier weather, this also blocks vitamin D absorption through the skin, so you can continue using the supplement year-round.

HOW MUCH MILK DOES MY TODDLER NEED?

In order to build up those little bones, your toddler needs the calcium in two full servings of dairy, so give your toddler a maximum of 2 cups of milk per day. If your child drinks more than this, their little tummy gets too full and your child will consume fewer solid foods. Too much milk can be a common cause of picky eaters.

Try to limit milk consumption to scheduled meals and snack times once your child is in this routine (at about one year) to protect their appetites and teeth. If your child does not like cow's milk, you can try fortified almond or hemp milk once they are two. But before age two, it's best to stick with breast milk or formula if they continue to refuse cow's milk. (But you can continue to offer it!)

You can also try different cups (a sippy cup, a cup with a straw, a cup with no lid) and different temperatures for the milk. Yogurt and cheese are also good sources of calcium but are not often fortified with vitamin D like fluid milk.

CAN I GIVE MY BABY ALMOND MILK?

Until age two, the only recommended milks for your baby include breast milk, formula, and whole cow's or goat's milk. Milk alternatives made from soy, almond, coconut, rice, and hemp are not high enough in protein or fat to meet your young child's needs. If your baby is under two years of age and sensitive to dairy, and you are no longer nursing, talk to your dietitian.

IS IT OKAY TO GIVE BABY WATER AND JUICE?

If your baby is less than six months old, breast milk or formula is the only fluid that baby requires. At six months, you can offer your baby small amounts of water, but it isn't necessary.

I would recommend waiting until one year of age to introduce juice, then offer a maximum of two to four ounces of 100 percent fruit juice per day, as part of a meal or snack. Fruit juice consumed at the same time as iron-containing foods can enhance iron absorption, since it contains vitamin C. There is no need to dilute the juice with water.

Remember, though, that too much juice can lead to diarrhea and early tooth decay, and it takes up belly space that healthier solids and milk would otherwise fill. And real fruit is always preferred, as it comes with fiber.

A new recommendation is to offer water only in an open cup, as sippy cups do not promote good oral motor development. Using an open cup also prevents extended use of bottles, which encourage excess caloric intake and are not great for teeth. Try using a small plastic Tupperware cup or an angled cup with handles, like the Doidy cup, and assist your little one in using it.

HOW SHOULD I DEAL WITH CONSTIPATION?

While babies don't often require extra fluid beyond milk, constipation is one situation where you might give your baby some water. Offer water in an open cup with meals, and this might be enough to help ease the constipation. You can also increase the amount of fiber in baby's diet. Fiber is the part of grains, fruits, vegetables, and legumes that is not digested. It makes stools easier to pass. High-fiber foods include:

- Beans and legumes
- Fruits and vegetables (pears, applesauce, peas, mixed vegetables)
- Whole grains

And don't forget about prunes, the great natural laxative! You can offer your baby 1 tablespoon strained prunes, increasing to ¼ cup per day if needed. As an alternative, make the Baby Lax recipe (page 98) I have included in this book, and serve your baby 1 tablespoon per day. It can be frozen in ice cube trays, just like homemade baby food, and mixed into cereal and yogurt or spread on toast.

If the increased fiber and prunes don't work on their own, add up to ½ cup fruit juice (pear, apple, or prune) per day, while continuing with the prunes. These fruits contain sorbitol, which draws water into the bowels to soften stools. Some babies may also find that an infant probiotic will help balance out their tummy bacteria and ease bowel movements.

ARE ORGANICS HEALTHIER?

People often ask whether organic food is healthier than conventional food. From a nutritional standpoint, there is little (if any) difference between organic and nonorganic dairy products and meats. But when it comes to produce, studies have shown that while they may not consistently be higher in vitamin content, organic fruits and vegetables contain more phytochemicals, which quench harmful free radicals in our bodies and may help prevent diseases like cancer.

Another reason to buy organic produce is to avoid pesticides. This is especially important for small children and pregnant and breastfeeding moms, as we still don't know what these chemicals may do to developing brains and bodies. That said, it is much better to eat conventional produce than none at all. If you can only afford to buy certain produce organic, organic apples and dried fruit are easy to find, and the conventional forms of these fruits contain lots of pesticides.[17]

Often, packaged organic food may appear healthier, but it is still heavily processed. Take a look at the ingredient list: "Organic brown rice syrup, organic corn syrup, organic honey"—all of this means sugar. And "organic unbleached flour" still means white flour. Don't trust the label just because it is green!

chapter 2
it's all about
the ingredients

All of the food we make at Baby Gourmet is organic. As I said in the previous chapter, when we're talking about nutritional value, little (if any) difference has been found between organic and conventional dairy products and meats. The primary difference lies in the addition of growth hormones and the use of antibiotics in the animals producing dairy. When it comes to produce, studies have shown that organic fruits and vegetables contain more phytochemicals than their conventional counterparts. Phytochemicals quench harmful free radicals in our bodies and may help prevent diseases like cancer, which is reason enough to encourage organic eating.

Another reason to buy organic produce is to avoid pesticides. This is especially important for small children and pregnant and breastfeeding moms, as we still don't know what these chemicals may do to developing brains and bodies. Not only do you avoid pesticides and genetically modified organisms when purchasing organic, but you also vote with your dollar, showing you support environmentally friendly farming practices that minimize soil erosion, safeguard workers, and protect water quality and wildlife.

I recommend buying organic whenever possible, but I also understand that organics are not accessible or affordable for everyone. If you can purchase only a few organic fruits and veggies, you should make sure to seek out organic versions of the following foods, which have the greatest risk of high concentrations of pesticide residue:

Apples	Spinach
Peaches	Sweet bell peppers
Nectarines	Cucumbers
Strawberries	Cherry tomatoes
Grapes	Potatoes
Celery	Kale

This is a list of produce that contains less pesticide residue, including:

Avocados	Papayas
Sweet corn	Kiwi
Pineapples	Eggplant
Cabbage	Grapefruit
Sweet peas, frozen	Cantaloupe
Onions	Cauliflower
Asparagus	Sweet potatoes
Mangoes	

WHAT ARE GMOS, AND HOW DO I KNOW IF THEY ARE IN MY FOOD?

Genetically modified organisms (GMOs) have been called Frankenfoods, and for good reason: To make them, a gene from one species is transferred to another, creating something that would not be found in nature. Because GMOs are relatively new to the market, the long-term effects of consuming them are yet to be known. I am sure many of you agree with the adage, "Better safe than sorry," and that pretty much sums up my take on whether I should allow my babies to be test subjects for these mutant crops.

To avoid GMOs, be sure to buy 100 percent certified organic products. You can also look for the symbol of the Non-GMO Project,[1] an organization that does the due diligence for you.

the basics

Now, at the beginning of your baby's journey, you are in a position to choose the highest-quality ingredients, full of all the essential nutrients to help your baby grow and develop. Complex carbohydrates, high-quality proteins, and good fats are the vital building blocks your baby needs for a strong, healthy body.

In this chapter, I am going to introduce some of my favorite ingredients to make the most nutritious and best tasting baby food. I have included some of the key nutritional benefits of each ingredient, how to buy and store it, and the best ways to use it.

WHOLE GRAINS AND SEEDS
Amaranth

The gluten-free super seed of the Aztecs is becoming very popular again in North America because of its wide variety of health benefits and its supply of essential vitamins and minerals, including B vitamins, calcium, iron, and zinc.

Amaranth is easy to digest and high in antioxidants. It helps in reducing anemia, possesses anti-inflammatory properties, and strengthens the immune system. This sweet and nutty-tasting seed is a complete protein containing all nine essential amino acids, and it's an excellent source of fiber and iron.

HOW TO BUY AND STORE: Amaranth looks like tiny quinoa and can be found in full seeds, flour, or puffed form, usually in the bulk section of your health food store. It is best to store amaranth in a tightly sealed container (preferably a glass jar) in a cool, dark, dry location. If stored properly, organic amaranth can have a shelf life of up to one year.

HOW TO USE: Amaranth can be cooked as porridge or added to bulk up a breakfast cereal. It also works well as an ingredient in soups and baking. I like to use it as a replacement for couscous or quinoa. Amaranth should be rinsed thoroughly under running water before cooking. To cook, mix ½ cup amaranth with 1½ cups water in a pot and bring to a boil. Reduce the heat to low and let it simmer uncovered for 20 to 25 minutes, until all of the water is absorbed.

Quinoa

"Gold of the Incas," quinoa is another powerhouse seed that looks and tastes like a grain. Gluten-free and full of essential vitamins and minerals, quinoa is a popular addition to baby's diet. It is a complete protein and high in antioxidants, with a high fiber content that supports digestion.

HOW TO BUY AND STORE: You can buy fresh quinoa in whole seed form, or if using for baking, you can purchase it as a flour or flake. Quinoa used to be found only in health food stores, but as testament to its growing popularity, supermarkets have started to carry it with increasing frequency. Store organic quinoa in sealed plastic or glass containers in a cool, dark, dry cabinet. Quinoa will stay fresh for up to one year if properly stored.

HOW TO USE: Quinoa can replace rice in most recipes and be used in soups, stir-fries, and casseroles. Try quinoa flour or flakes in porridges, smoothies, and baked goods. Cooking quinoa seeds is really easy—just combine 1 cup quinoa with 2 cups water and bring the mixture to a boil. Reduce the heat, cover, and simmer for 15 to 20 minutes. Fluff it with a fork, and it's ready to serve. Quinoa should be rinsed thoroughly under running water before cooking.

Barley

Barley is a great baby food, as it is easily blended into purees, and soft, cooked barley can be a great finger food for little pinchers. Barley contains amino acids, lots of fiber (ounce for ounce, three times as much fiber as oatmeal), B vitamins, iron, selenium, copper, manganese, and phosphorus—all essential nutrients for baby's development. Note, however, that you should be extra careful about introducing barley if your baby is allergic to wheat, as there may be a relationship between barley allergy (which is quite rare) and wheat allergy.

HOW TO BUY AND STORE: There are many different forms of barley to choose from, such as pearled, hulled, flour, or flakes. Hulled, although minimally processed, is a little tougher and chewier than the other forms. Pearl barley refers to covered barley that has been processed to remove the tough inedible outer hull. It is usually found next to dry beans, lentils, and rice. Pearl barley may also be found in bulk containers in the natural food sections of supermarkets, as well as in health and specialty food stores. Raw barley should be stored in an airtight container in a cool place, preferably the refrigerator or freezer, where it will keep for about six months.

HOW TO USE: Barley is incredibly versatile and can be used to make breakfast, savory dishes, and even dessert! You can use it to bulk up soups and stews, making them more satisfying as well as more nutritious, or you can simply serve it as a side dish instead of rice or pasta. With pearl barley, the general rule is to use 1 cup of barley to 2 cups of water. Bring the water to a rolling boil, then add the barley. Bring the liquid back to a boil, then lower the heat and simmer for about 40 minutes. Pearl barley takes around an hour to cook, and hulled barley takes around 1½ hours.

If you want your baby's barley to cook faster and be easier to digest, try soaking it first, which not only increases its digestibility but also makes its nutrients more bioavailable (easy for the body to absorb). To do this, place the desired amount of barley in a bowl and cover with twice as much water. Let it soak for several hours (or just leave it overnight), then drain and rinse.

Brown Rice

A common first food because of its low allergen rates and ease of digestion, brown rice makes a wonderful ground baby cereal and is great for introducing texture to developing palates. Brown rice is very nutritious with excellent sources of B vitamins, manganese, selenium, iron, and fiber. I would choose brown rice over white rice, because brown rice is not highly processed and stripped of its natural goodness.

HOW TO BUY AND STORE: Because brown rice contains the healthy natural oils of the germ, it has a shelf life of about six months—far shorter than that of refined white rice—although that time can be extended by an additional six months if the rice is refrigerated. Check for usability dates on packages or, when buying in bulk, do so from a busy store with a high turnover.

HOW TO USE: Grind brown rice into powder to make baby's first cereal, or add it to purees to provide a soft texture as baby learns to chew, as it works with both savory and sweet dishes. Brown rice takes a little longer to cook than other grains. Combine 1 cup rice with 1½ cups water and bring the mixture to a boil. Then reduce the heat, cover, and simmer for 40 to 50 minutes. Let stand 5 minutes, then fluff it with a fork. Always rinse and drain rice before cooking.

Spelt

Like quinoa, millet, and amaranth, spelt is an ancient grain that has so far avoided mass manipulation by industrial agriculture. It's a cereal grain in the wheat family, but it is not the same thing as wheat—same genus, different species. While spelt does contain gluten, it is a water-soluble gluten, unlike that of its cousin. This makes spelt much easier to digest than wheat, but those with celiac disease should avoid it, too. Spelt is an excellent source of vitamin B_2, a very good source of manganese, and a good source of niacin, thiamine, copper, and fiber. Another plus: Spelt has more protein than wheat.

HOW TO BUY AND STORE: Store spelt flour and flakes in sealed containers in a cool, dark, dry cabinet. Spelt will stay fresh for up to one year if properly stored.

HOW TO USE: Spelt flour can replace white, whole wheat, or whole grain flour in recipes for breads and baked goods. Spelt pasta can be purchased as whole grain or white, with whole grain being higher in protein and fiber. White spelt flour is more refined, has lower gluten levels, and is easier to bake with.

Oats

Oats are one of the quintessential nutrient-dense first foods in baby's diet. They are an excellent source of soluble fiber, protein, and the B vitamins thiamine, riboflavin, and B_6. They also provide iron, magnesium, selenium, and phosphorus.

Best of all, they help to stabilize blood sugar levels, keeping baby calm and full of energy. All forms of oats are whole grain. Even when oats are processed to make quick-cooking versions, the entire grain remains intact. This means they retain all the goodness contained in the germ, endosperm, and bran—and that's a lot of goodness! Oats do contain a little of the glutenin and gliadin that make up gluten and are associated with the potential development of celiac disease. This is more by the circumstances of their growth than by nature: Pure oats don't contain gluten, although oats may be contaminated by other glutenous grains (like wheat, barley, and rye) with which they are grown, harvested, processed, or stored.

HOW TO BUY AND STORE: Buy small quantities of oats at one time since this grain has a slightly higher fat content than other grains and can spoil more quickly. It is best to store whole oats in an airtight container in a cool, dry, and dark place, where they will keep for up to six months.

HOW TO USE: It's very easy to grind your own oats to make oatmeal cereal with the creamy texture babies love. Alternatively, you can cook whole oats and add them to a variety of dishes. Finely ground oats make a super healthy thickener for soups, overly runny purees, and sauces. Save time in the mornings by cooking your oats the night before and warming them up at breakfast time. You can even cook several days' supply in one go and store it in the refrigerator, warming portions

as needed. If you're really pressed for time, prepared oatmeal can be frozen for later use. For old-fashioned rolled oats, bring ½ cup oats and 1 cup water to a boil, reduce the heat, cover, and simmer for about 5 minutes. Earthier steel cut oats take longer and require more water. Bring 3½ cups water to a boil and add ½ cup steel cut oats. Reduce the heat, cover, and simmer for 25 to 30 minutes.

Millet

Millet provides a host of nutrients, has a sweet, nutty flavor, and is considered to be one of the most digestible and nonallergenic grains available. This high-protein, high-fiber, gluten-free grain is rich in B vitamins, potassium, phosphorus, magnesium, and iron.

HOW TO BUY AND STORE: Whole grain millet is best stored in a tightly sealed container, preferably a glass jar, in a cool, dark, dry location. Stored properly, millet can have a shelf life of up to one year.

HOW TO USE: Millet is very easy to prepare and can be made in several different ways to suit your baby's changing needs as baby grows. You can start off by grinding up the grains to make a cereal. After baby gets a bit older, you can start to cook it whole, preparing it the same way you do other grains such as amaranth, quinoa, rice, and barley. Like all grains, millet should be rinsed thoroughly under running water before cooking. After rinsing, add 1 cup millet to 2½ cups water. When it comes to a boil, reduce the heat, cover, and simmer for about 25 minutes. The texture of millet cooked this way will be fluffy like rice. If you want a creamier consistency, stir it frequently, adding a little more water every now and then.

Coconut Milk

Made from crushing and squeezing the meat of a coconut, coconut milk is one of my favorite ways to add creaminess to any dish. Your baby does not need to be dairy- or lactose-intolerant to enjoy all the health benefits of this superfood. Coconut milk contains immunity-boosting lauric acid, which is found heavily in breast milk, making coconut milk a great addition to your child's diet. People are sometimes confused as to whether a coconut is a nut or a seed—in fact, it is a fruit from the palm family and not a tree nut, so coconut allergies are relatively low. That said, as with any new food, be sure to watch for reactions and discuss with your pediatrician if you're concerned.

HOW TO BUY AND STORE: I prefer canned or home-made coconut milk, as it has a much creamier consistency without all the added preservatives and stabilizers you'll find in the refrigerated version. When shopping for coconut milk, look for BPA-free cans. My favorite brand is Native Forest, which is organic and BPA-free.

HOW TO USE: Coconut milk is a wonderful dairy alternative and can be used to replace cow's milk in many recipes. I use coconut milk when making soups, sauces, smoothies, and baked goods—your imagination's the limit!

Flax Seeds

Flax seeds provide baby with a vegetarian source of omega-3 fatty acids, along with calcium and phosphorus, which promote bone development. As if that weren't enough of a reason to incorporate them into your recipes, they also help reduce baby's risk of anemia with a good supply of iron and act as a natural laxative thanks to their high dietary fiber. The risk of an allergic reaction to flax seeds is very low.

HOW TO BUY AND STORE: When purchasing flax seeds, color counts: The darker the seed, the higher the omega-3 content. You can also purchase flax meal, which is pre-ground and ready for use. Flax meal should come in a vacuum-sealed package and be stored in the freezer once opened to prevent rancidity.

HOW TO USE: In order for these powerhouse seeds to be digestible, they need to be boiled and mashed into a paste, ground in a grinder as needed, or purchased as flax meal. Eat the seeds whole, and they'll simply pass through your system undigested. Add flax meal to baking, stir into your porridge or yogurt, or use in lieu of breadcrumbs.

Chia

Native to South America, chia seeds have been around for centuries, but only in the last few years have their health benefits made them popular in North America. Chia seeds are rich in nutrients and antioxidants and have high levels of ALA omega-3—in fact, chia seeds are one of the best plant-based sources of fatty acids. Because it's so high in fiber, chia helps regulate bowels, which is very important, as babies can get constipated easily.

HOW TO BUY AND STORE: Chia seeds can be purchased whole or ground and are either white or black in color. The difference between the two colors is negligible—both contain essentially the same amount of omega-3, protein, fiber, and other nutrients. Unlike flax seeds, chia seeds do not need to be ground for proper absorption. Whole chia seeds will stay in good condition at room temperature for several years; their natural antioxidants provide this stability. Storing chia in a closed container will help extend its shelf life.

HOW TO USE: Because of how its outer seed layer absorbs liquids, chia seeds can be used to thicken recipes and give them a bit of crunch, similar to that of small tapioca beads. Some people use chia as an egg substitute for babies who are allergic to or intolerant of eggs. All you need to do is mix 1 tablespoon of chia seeds with 3 tablespoons of water and let it sit for 15 minutes. It should have a slightly jellylike consistency. Chia can be used in baking or added to baby's favorite purees for an extra nutrition boost. If babies spit out the seeds served whole, then try blending seeds with the purees. You can even purchase ground chia seeds.

Hemp

Including hemp in your child's diet is one of the healthiest things you could do for them. Not only is hemp a good source of protein, but it is also one of only a few plant foods that provide all of the essential amino acids, making it a complete protein. Hemp also offers the perfect balance of omega-3 to omega-6 fatty acids.

HOW TO BUY AND STORE: You can purchase hemp in a number of incarnations: hemp oil, hulled hearts (also called hemp seeds), or protein powders. For cooking I prefer hemp oil and hearts, as the protein powder tends to have a strong flavor. Hemp hearts are best stored in the fridge or freezer for extended shelf life. You can store unopened hemp seeds in a cool, dark place for a year; once opened, they last eight weeks. Hemp oil must be refrigerated.

HOW TO USE: With their light and nutty flavor, hemp seeds are easily incorporated into baked goods and smoothies. They work well blended into purees, yogurt, soups, and hot cereals.

BEANS AND LEGUMES
Black Beans

Black beans are a major source of carbohydrates, protein, and fiber. They are also filled with important nutrients, including iron, calcium, and folate, which help nourish your baby's growing body.

HOW TO BUY AND STORE: Black beans are available in two forms, dry and canned. Dry beans are much more cost-effective and much lower in sodium. Canned beans are more convenient. If you decide to go for canned beans, look for the ones that are low or reduced sodium. Store dry beans in airtight containers and use them within one year of purchase.

Store canned beans in cool cabinets and use them within one year of purchase.

HOW TO USE: For younger babies, puree black beans with a bit of liquid, then add to a sweet puree like bananas, carrots, or sweet potatoes for a protein- and fiber-packed meal. For older babies, cooked beans are easy to eat whole. Try adding whole cooked beans to soups and rice and pasta dishes. To ease digestion, it is best to soak and cook your beans well, allowing them to break down more easily. If you're cooking them from their dried state, soak them for 12 to 24 hours, then drain and rinse. Bring a full pot of water and beans to a boil, reduce the heat to low, and cook anywhere from 60 to 90 minutes. Beans should be tender but not mushy. Canned beans are a quick and easy option; however, it is best to look for ones that contain no or low salt. Always rinse canned beans before using.

Chickpeas (Garbanzo Beans)

Chickpeas are a great source of fiber, folic acid, iron, and protein. These nutrients are key: They reduce the risk of anemia, support bone growth, promote healthy digestion, and improve lower intestinal tract functionality. Chickpeas are also a good source of polyunsaturated fats.

HOW TO BUY AND STORE: Chickpeas can be bought dried or canned and found in grocery stores. Look for chickpeas in the ethnic, bulk, or canned food sections. It is best to use dried chickpeas within a year of buying them. The longer they are stored, the drier they become, which increases the cook-ing time. Canned chickpeas are very convenient as they are ready-to-use. Avoid cans of chickpeas that are dented, leaking, or cracked with bulging lids. Store canned chickpeas in a cool, dry place. Make sure to rinse canned chickpeas well to lower the sodium content.

HOW TO USE: For younger babies, puree chickpeas with a bit of liquid and add them to a yummy fruit or veggie puree for a protein- and fiber-packed meal. Mash them up with a touch of olive oil, lemon juice, tahini, salt, and pepper for a delicious hummus that can be used as a dip or spread. For older babies, cooked chickpeas are soft and easy to eat whole. Try adding whole cooked beans to soups, pastas, and grain or seed dishes for texture.

Lentils

Don't underestimate the humble lentil. Despite its small size, this little legume offers huge benefits for your baby. Lentils are high in protein, folate, potassium, calcium, phosphorus, fiber, and iron. Collectively, these nutrients help to build your baby's immune, skeletal, and muscular-vascular systems, as well as enhancing brain development. Like most beans and legumes, lentils sometimes give babies gas, so they should be introduced slowly into your little one's diet.

HOW TO BUY AND STORE: Dried lentils often cost less than canned ones, but canned lentils are still a good buy and can save you a lot of time. Just open the can, rinse for a few minutes, and add them to your dish. Store dried lentils in an airtight container in the cupboard or a cool, dry place for up to one year. Dried lentils that have been cooked can be kept covered in the fridge for five to seven days or frozen for up to six months. Label with the date and store them in an airtight container made for freezing food. Having lentils in the freezer makes them easy to add to any meal. Unopened canned lentils will keep in the cupboard or a cool, dry place for up to one year. After opening and rinsing canned lentils, store them in a covered glass or airtight container in the fridge, not in the opened can. They will keep for three to four days.

HOW TO USE: When preparing lentils, begin by rinsing them in cold water. Lentils cook to a mushier consistency than most other beans and vegetables, making them easier for your baby to eat and digest. For a younger baby, mash cooked lentils with a fruit or veggie puree, or mix whole cooked lentils into your baby's veggie puree for added texture. Lentils are also the perfect "thickener" for purees, soups, or casseroles, and they go well with fruits and veggies.

Apples

Apples are the most popular fruit in the world, and for good reason! I love to use apples in my recipes because they are so versatile, easy to prepare, easy to digest, and full of nutrients. Apples are rich in antioxidants, immunity-boosting vitamin C, and fiber, as well as trace mineral boron, which is essential to strengthening bones. Remember: The apple peel hosts most of these magnificent properties, so always keep the skin on the apple.

HOW TO BUY AND STORE: Because apples are on the top of EWG's "dirty dozen" list of produce with high pesticide residues, and we want to keep all the goodness of the apple peel, I always recommend buying organic apples, firm and unblemished. For babies, the less tart and less acidic apples are best. I would look for Gala, Golden Delicious, Braeburn, Empire, or Honeycrisp. Once you get your apples home, store them on the counter for maximum taste and freshness. If you don't get around to eating them within a few days, you can throw them in the fridge to extend their life span a little longer.

HOW TO USE: Applesauce is a wonderfully delicious base for any puree. I like to use it with a protein puree, such as chicken, turkey, pork, or fish. It also tastes great combined with veggies, grains, and other fruits, or as a substitute for oil, butter, or eggs when baking. Paired with cheese or peanut butter, apples make a delicious snack for older babies.

Pears

Like apples, pears are versatile, easy to digest, and full of valuable nutrients. My kids still love pears—they're their fruit of choice when grabbing something out of the fruit bowl. It's no wonder: Pears have a distinct texture and, when ripe, are so sweet and succulent. Rich in antioxidants, fiber, and antimicrobial properties, pear is a wonderful fruit for baby.

HOW TO BUY AND STORE: Look for ripe, unblemished pears—the riper, the juicier! Store them on the counter to ripen them more quickly, then put them into the refrigerator to extend their shelf life a couple of days.

HOW TO USE: Puree pears on their own for a simple treat or add to pureed veggies to enhance the flavor. They taste delicious blended with steamed greens such as broccoli and spinach. Ripe pears diced into bite-size pieces make a great finger food for babies learning to feed themselves.

Bananas

Where to begin with the benefits of eating bananas? Nutrient-packed and easy on baby's belly, bananas are the perfect combination of health, taste, and ease. Portable, easily sourced, and just as easy to prepare, they're the ultimate convenience food for baby. Bananas are rich in nutrients such as potassium and have an abundance of vitamins, particularly vitamin B_6, vitamin C, and vitamin B_2. These are essential nutrients needed during the first months of baby's development. But don't forget that you can get too much of a good thing: Too many bananas may lead to constipation.

HOW TO BUY AND STORE: Select bananas from the store that are yellow to yellow-green in color, without too many black spots. The banana is ready for your baby when most of the green has turned yellow, and the banana peel pulls away with ease. Store bananas in their peel at room temperature. If bananas become overripe, then throw them in

the freezer and use them for smoothies. Unripe banana should not be given to your baby, as it is very hard to digest. Note that bananas will suffer from browning once prepared. This is perfectly normal and still fine for your baby to eat.

HOW TO USE: Bananas can be eaten directly from the peel, mashed and served, or diced into bite-size pieces for finger food. I like to use bananas as a base for many recipes because of the creamy texture and naturally sweet flavor. I also use mashed bananas in a number of baking recipes to replace fat and sugar content.

Mangoes

In the tropics, the mango wears the crown of the "King of Fruits." And for good reason! Aside from being delicious, mangoes are also one of the healthiest fruits for your baby, as they contain high amounts of vitamins, minerals, and carbohydrates. Eating mangoes may help protect eyesight, as they are an excellent source of vitamin A and flavonoids like beta-carotene, alpha-carotene, and beta-cryptoxanthin. They can also ease digestion and increase immunity.

HOW TO BUY AND STORE: Look for ripe mangoes that give slightly when pressed with your fingers. Avoid mangoes that are rock hard or too mushy and mangoes with skin that has begun to wrinkle, as these could be overripe. Choose mangoes that are slightly more round and plump, rather than flat. Definitely don't judge a mango by its color! Mangoes come in so many color variations, and no one is necessarily better than another.

If you do bring home a mango that's slightly firmer to the touch and not quite ready to go, ripening is easy! Just leave the mango out at room temperature until it has the signs of ripeness mentioned above. Or, to speed up the process, let the mango ripen inside a paper bag (also at room temperature).

HOW TO USE: Mangoes contain fibers, which can make swallowing difficult for baby. If you have a fibrous mango, puree it or add it to a smoothie. Fresh mangoes can be enjoyed on their own. For older babies, dice a mango into bite-size pieces for finger food, or add it to smoothies, savory dishes, or desserts like rice pudding and yogurt. Do not feed unripe mangoes to baby—not only do they taste sour, but they are also difficult to digest.

Berries

Whether we are talking about blueberries, raspberries, strawberries, or blackberries, all these delicious morsels burst with flavor and nutrients. Colorful berries are high in antioxidants and a good source of fiber, potassium, and vitamin C. Vitamin C helps prevent infection and boosts the immune system, and potassium supports a healthy heart and iron for red blood cells.

HOW TO BUY AND STORE: Berries are among the "dirty dozen" foods that are most highly contaminated with pesticides, so purchasing organic is important. When selecting berries, look for those that are deeply colored and not bruised or overly squishy. To store berries, refrigerate loosely covered. Because berries are so delicate, do not wash them until right before use. Properly stored, berries will maintain their freshness for up to two weeks in the refrigerator. To freeze berries, rinse, pat dry, and arrange laying flat on a baking sheet. Freeze until solid and then transfer to a resealable bag or freezer container for easy access. You can store them in the freezer for up to three months.

HOW TO USE: Diced berries are a healthy stand-alone snack for an older baby, and incorporating them into meals is a simple way to boost baby's antioxidant and nutrient intake. But served whole, berries are a choking hazard, so be sure to cut them into small pieces. Give them to baby with oatmeal, alongside sliced turkey and shredded cheese, or blended with a bit of yogurt to make a tasty smoothie. I suggest stewing berries before pureeing them for easier digestion.

Avocados

Aside from being one of my favorite foods, avocados are also one of the easiest and healthiest first foods for baby. Avocados are an excellent source of fiber and potassium, and they're rich in vitamins K, B, C, and E. An avocado's creamy texture comes from all its healthy fats, and for a fruit, it actually has a decent amount of protein.

HOW TO BUY AND STORE: Avocados are ripe when they have some give when you squeeze their skin—not too much give, though, as this means the avocado has spoiled. Look for ones without blemishes. If you purchase them still firm, simply leave them on the counter until they ripen. If they ripen too soon, put them in the fridge until you are ready to consume them. If you use only half the avocado, store the remaining half in the fridge with the seed still inside the flesh. The seed helps keep the avocado from turning brown.

HOW TO USE: Mash it into a puree, dice it into cubes, spread it on toast, or blend it into a smoothie. Because there is no cooking and very little preparation required, you can feed an avocado to baby straight from the peel. You'll find few foods as healthy and convenient for baby.

Broccoli

The official first food I made for my babies, broccoli is a staple in our household and remains my kids' favorite veggie to this day. Broccoli seems to be one of those vegetables that elicits a love-hate response, but let's try to develop a love for it, because it is simply brimming with key nutrients. The benefits of eating broccoli are enormous—it could hardly be healthier! A serving of broccoli has more vitamin C than an orange, and vitamin C helps the body absorb iron from other foods. It also boosts baby's immune system and has anti-inflammatory properties. And that's not even to begin to talk about broccoli's phytonutrients, one of which—sulforaphane—has attracted scientific attention as a potential cancer fighter.

HOW TO BUY AND STORE: Choose broccoli heads with tight, green florets and firm stalks. The broccoli should feel heavy for its size. The cut ends of the stalks should be fresh and look moist. Avoid broccoli with dried or browning stem ends or yel-

lowing florets. Store broccoli unwashed in an open plastic bag in the refrigerator. If bought very fresh, broccoli will keep up to ten days.

HOW TO USE: I believe that much of your baby's response to broccoli will depend on how you prepare it. Overcooking broccoli brings out strong, unappetizing flavors and smells. It loses its texture, and the color turns a brownish green, which is not doing the poor broccoli (or your baby) any favors. A gentle steam to fork-tender will create a fresh, bright green puree that baby will find appealing. If they refuse, keep trying. This is one of those foods you do not want to give up on. Try mixing it with mashed banana or sweet potato for added sweetness, or avocado for a creamier texture.

Sweet Potatoes and Yams

A classic baby favorite and ideal first food, sweet potatoes and yams are rich in both flavor and nutrients. Go to any supermarket and you're almost guaranteed to find one or the other. And let me go on: They are easy to prepare, easy to digest, and easy on the taste buds! Sweet potatoes contain lots of dietary fiber and beta-carotene, calcium, iron, vitamin A, vitamin C, and even vitamin E. Low on the glycemic index, sweet potatoes digest slowly, so they won't spike baby's blood sugar.

HOW TO BUY AND STORE: Sweet potatoes and yams are available year-round, but their peak growing season is fall. Look for sweet potatoes or yams that are firm and free of cracks or soft spots.

Though you can find them in either orange or white tones, I opt for the orange ones, as they are more beta-carotene dense. If stored in a dark pantry, sweet potatoes and yams can keep for weeks.

HOW TO USE: For maximum flavor, roast or bake sweet potatoes and yams, but you can cube and boil them when in a pinch for time. Try substituting sweet potatoes or yams in recipes that call for regular potatoes. Mashed cooked sweet potatoes taste yummy on their own, but add a little butter, olive oil, or coconut oil and a pinch of cinnamon or ground sage for something a little bit different. I like to use sweet potato and yam puree as a base and then add pureed meats and vegetables to create more complex meals.

Pumpkin

Pumpkins shouldn't be relegated to Halloween. They make a wonderful baby food year-round and a delicious addition to baked goods for the whole family. Pumpkin provides fiber, antioxidants, vitamin A, and essential nutrients for baby's development; it also builds a stronger immune system and has antimicrobial properties.

HOW TO BUY AND STORE: The secret to selecting the best pumpkin lies in assessing its color, texture, and overall appearance. A good pumpkin will be firm to the touch, without any soft spots or cuts. It must be orange in color. When picking pumpkins for eating, it's better to purchase smaller pie pumpkins than the large jack-o'-lantern pumpkins as not only are they easier to prepare, but they're also much sweeter.

HOW TO USE: After you have cleaned the pumpkin thoroughly on the outside, you can either steam or roast the pumpkin. If you are steaming, peel it, seed it, and cut it into cubes. If roasting, you do not need to peel the pumpkin—simply cut it in half, seed it, and roast. Remove the flesh from the peel prior to processing. Pumpkin puree is great on its own, but I also use it generously in my baking. Who doesn't love freshly baked pumpkin muffins?

Carrots

What makes carrots a good choice for babies? Simple: They're easy to digest, pleasant to taste, and packed full of nutrients such as beta-carotene, folate, and vitamin C. Beta-carotene is converted to vitamin A, and the abundance of it in carrots makes this ubiquitous veggie a great one. Fat-soluble vitamin A plays an essential role in vision, growth, and development; the maintenance of healthy skin, hair, and mucous membranes; and immune functions. It is the high level of beta-carotene that causes carrots to be colored orange, and this may also cause baby's skin to take on an orange glow. Fear not, parents: If your baby develops an orange glow, just cut back on the servings of beta-carotene-rich foods, and you'll see the normal skin color return.

HOW TO BUY AND STORE: Carrots are abundant and readily available no matter what season. Look for smooth, firm, and crisp carrots with deep color and fresh green tops (if present). Avoid carrots that are split, wilted, or sprouting, as this indicates

that they are old. Remove tops (if present) and refrigerate carrots in a crisper.

HOW TO USE: Do not wash carrots until you are ready to use them. Gently scrub them under cold water to wash off any excess dirt. Peel if desired. They are very simple to prepare by either steaming or roasting. Puree for young babies, or dice into bite-size pieces and cook for a soft finger food.

Butternut Squash

Butternut squash, with its elongated pear shape, light tan color, and deep orange flesh is the most popular winter squash. Its sweet, smooth, and nutty flavor makes a delicious soup for you and will make an equally delicious puree for baby. Butternut squash has many vital polyphenolic antioxidants and vitamins. It has more vitamin A than a pumpkin. Vitamin A is a powerful natural antioxidant and is required by the body for maintaining the integrity of skin and mucous membranes. It is also an essential vitamin for optimal eyesight. It is rich in B-complex vitamins like folate, niacin, vitamin B_6 (pyridoxine), and thiamine. Butternut squash is also a good source of dietary fiber and phytonutrients.

HOW TO BUY AND STORE: Select a butternut squash that has an even cream color and is firm and heavy for its size. Avoid squash that has soft spots, is dull, has wrinkled skin, or is light for its size. Winter squash typically may be stored for a long period of time. Depending on the variety, a winter squash such as butternut may be stored for up to four months. Store your winter squash in a cool, dry place for optimal storage. Once cut open, cover and refrigerate for up to five days.

HOW TO USE: The best way to cook butternut squash is to bake or roast it. This retains the most nutrients while bringing out the most flavor. With a sharp kitchen knife, cut the butternut squash in half lengthwise. Scoop out the seeds from the round end of the cut butternut squash. Lay the butternut squash halves cut side down in a baking dish in 1 to 2 inches of water. Bake at 400°F for 40 minutes or until the skin looks puckery and turns a darker tan. If you are looking to roast bite-sized pieces, simply peel and dice the squash, toss with a little olive oil, and roast with the same instructions above.

Green Beans

High in calcium, vitamin K, and vitamin C, green beans are another great source of nutrients for baby. Although their fibrous texture is a bit difficult to make into a smooth puree, blending them with creamy sweet potatoes, avocados, or bananas can help. There is really nothing better than a fresh green bean gently steamed and cut into bite-size pieces for new self-feeders, and it ranks very low on the list of foods that prompt allergic reactions.

HOW TO BUY AND STORE: When purchasing fresh green beans, look for firm beans without any blemishes or squishy parts. Fresh green beans will keep in the refrigerator for up to five days. Store them in a plastic bag in the crisper bin. Do not wash, trim, or cut fresh green beans until you are ready to use them.

HOW TO USE: Green beans are best when steamed or boiled gently. Let 1 inch of water come to a boil, and then add the green beans. Cook the green beans uncovered for a few minutes, then cover for 6 to 12 minutes—shorter for adult consumption and longer for baby's puree. Because of green beans' tough skin, you may need to use a food mill to break them down completely for a smooth puree.

Peas

Sweet green peas, although deceptively small, are one of the most nutritious leguminous vegetables, rich in phytonutrients, antioxidants, minerals like calcium, and vitamins such as folate and vitamins A, C, and K. Fresh or frozen, peas are readily available and an easy addition to most meals.

HOW TO BUY AND STORE: When selecting fresh green peas, check the pod carefully. You're looking for medium-size pods containing peas that are firm and crisp, with a bright green color. Avoid tough, thick-skinned pods, as this is an indication that the peas are overmatured, as well as those that exhibit poor color or show any sign of decay or wilting. When you bring green peas home from the market, remember that they have a very short shelf life, so use them right away. If out of season, frozen is the next best thing and readily available.

HOW TO USE: Steaming or boiling peas in a scant amount of water is the best way to cook peas for baby food. If making a puree, you may need to use a food mill to break down the tough skin completely. Alternatively, cooked peas make a wonderful self-feeding food because of their small size and soft, mushy texture.

Spinach

Spinach is a hero when it comes to providing vitamins and minerals for baby's growth and development. It supplies some of the most essential minerals such as calcium, magnesium, iron, and potassium. Spinach's vitamins A, C, and K, thiamine, riboflavin, folate, and niacin all play important roles in improving bodily function. Just when you thought you could not get any more benefits, spinach also contains antimicrobial properties and a significant amount of dietary fiber. Go, spinach!

HOW TO BUY AND STORE: The texture of spinach leaves is very important while choosing the best for your baby. Spinach leaves must be bright green and firm without any tears, wrinkles, or darkening. Store washed and dried spinach in a resealable bag lined with paper towels for up to three weeks. Be sure to dry it carefully, as excess moisture will cause rotting.

HOW TO USE: Steaming or gently sautéing is the best way to preserve the nutrients in spinach. Pureed spinach rarely goes over well with baby because of its strong flavor. I recommend a three-to-one ratio between fruit/veg and spinach. Mixing at this ratio softens the flavor while still getting all those great nutrients into baby. For the rest of the family, I also chop spinach and add it to soups or smoothies as often as possible.

Kale

Like spinach, this dark leafy green has many key nutrients for baby's development. High in vitamins like folate, minerals like iron, and antioxidants, kale also contains fiber, protein, and omega-3s. No wonder it's considered a superfood! Kale is not a natural baby favorite, but combine it with other softer flavors, and it'll be a great addition to baby's diet.

HOW TO BUY AND STORE: Kale leaves should be firm and deeply colored with stems that are moist and strong. Make sure that the leaves are not browning or yellowing and that they are free of small holes. Avoid wilted leaves, as this is an indication that the greens have been sitting on the shelf for too long or that they were not properly stored. Kale should be refrigerated in an airtight bag. It can typically be stored for up to five days, but you may notice the flavor increases in bitterness with longer storage. Wash the kale only when you are ready to use it, as washing before storage promotes spoilage.

HOW TO USE: Kale has a very powerful flavor and thick texture that do not make it very appealing on its own. I highly recommend steaming and pureeing it until smooth and then adding it to other puree combinations such as apples or bananas to soften the flavor. I also recommend adding it into smoothies, chopping it into stews, or baking it into chips for a tasty toddler-friendly snack.

Fennel

Fennel bulbs are funky-looking roots that smell and taste like anise. I feel fennel is underused. Not only is it equally delicious raw or cooked, but it's also great for much of what might ail babies' bellies and can ease indigestion, constipation, and flatulence. It's also a very rich source of potassium, an essential nutrient required for blood pressure and muscle contraction.

HOW TO BUY AND STORE: Select small to medium white bulbs that are heavy and firm with bright green feathery fronds. Avoid bulbs that are really large, have moist spots, or appear shriveled and dried out. Bulbs and stalks should be free of cracks, splits, and any discoloration or bruising. As with carrots, if you're storing fennel in the fridge, you'll want to separate the stalks from the bulb and store the two parts separately in plastic bags. Try to use your fennel within a few days—any more than that, and it starts to lose flavor.

HOW TO USE: Roasting fennel for your baby purees is the best way to bring out its natural sweetness and soften its flavor. It tastes wonderful spiced with a pinch of cinnamon or nutmeg and is delicious blended with most fruits, veggies, and proteins. When baby gets older, raw fennel is a must on your veggie tray.

PROTEINS

I believe baby should have the purest, most wholesome foods whenever possible, so when it comes to choosing the best meat, look for either organic or naturally raised, grass-fed, grass-finished beef. Most of the guidelines below refer to U.S. standards, but I have made note of Canadian variations and resources as well.

Organic, All-Natural, or Naturally Raised Meat: What Are the Differences?

ORGANICALLY LABELED meat means that the animal's diet can consist of any grain or forage product as long as those feed items are certified organic. This program is the strictest, with the most guidelines, and is governed by the USDA's National Organic Program (NOP). To be certified organic, a grain or forage resource must not have had synthetic fertilizers, sewage sludge, irradiation, or genetically engineered products produced on that ground in three or more years. Additionally, the livestock cannot receive antibiotics or growth hormones. The important thing to keep in mind here is that organic refers only to what the animal has consumed. The NOP does not regulate or govern what happens to the meat during processing. This means the final product can be altered with additional colorants or spices, sauces, and the like. That said, any additives would also have to be organic if the product is to be labeled organic.

"Organic" is the most highly regulated label and the most difficult for producers to achieve. It's defined more stringently than other label claims, like "natural," which are mostly marketing. In Canada, each province may have its own standards for organic meat.[2] But the criteria are similar to the U.S. wording:

> Organic meat comes from an animal that has not been fed anything grown with toxic or synthetic fertilizers, pesticides, herbicides, fungicides, or fumigants; has not been given any kind of growth hormone, antibiotic, or genetically engineered product; has been conceived by organically raised animals; and has been butchered and processed following organic regulations. Organically raised animals are provided with living conditions and stocking rates appropriate to their behavioral requirements, high-quality diet of organically produced feed, and ethical animal husbandry that facilitates low stress, promotes good health, and prevents disease. With organic farming, prevention of maladies is emphasized over treatment of them.[3]

ALL-NATURAL LABELED meat, poultry, and eggs cannot be altered during processing; this would include the addition of artificial ingredients (spices, marinades, sauces, etc.), colorants, or chemical preservatives, so the meat is minimally processed. That said, all-natural does not include any standards for farm practices. It is a common myth that animals bred to become all-natural meat cannot receive growth hormones or antibiotics—the truth is that each individual producer decides whether their animals will receive growth hormones and/or antibiotics. Additionally, there are no regulations regarding what the animals can or cannot consume. Meat labeled as all-natural can come from an animal that has consumed any grain or forage product, whether that grain or forage was organic or not. Unlike organically labeled meats, there is no governing body for all-natural meat products.

NATURALLY RAISED—not to be confused with all-natural—means that livestock used for the production of meat and meat products have been raised entirely without additional growth hormones, antibiotics, or animal by-products. Naturally raised does have a certification program, and all products must be certified by the USDA's Agricultural Marketing Service (AMS). This meat does not contain any artificial ingredients, colorants, or chemicals, making it minimally processed.

In Canada, "natural" and "naturally raised" refer to the same standards. According to the Canadian Food Inspection Agency's website: With respect to a meat, poultry, or fish product, "natural" and "naturally raised" claims are considered acceptable only on products that were raised with minimal human intervention, for example, wild turkey or wild fish. To raise animals so that their products can be labeled as "natural" would be very difficult as most animals receive vaccination or medication and the feed given usually contains vitamins, minerals, additives, medication, and direct-fed microbials, none of which are considered to be minimal human interventions. To claim on a product label "naturally raised" would be even more difficult, as raising a farm animal or fish is an expression of human intervention.

When a "natural" or "naturally raised" claim cannot be made, there may be other, more specific claims which convey information on the methods used to raise a particular animal or fish, provided they are truthful and not misleading; for example, "grain fed," "raised without the use of antibiotics," or "raised without the use of hormones."[4]

GRASS-FED OR GRASS-FINISHED means the animals have been fed an exclusively grass diet, from beginning to end. They are not given grains (usually corn or soy) or animal by-products. Eating grass maintains the animals' digestive health. The alternative is grain-fed and grain-finished. According to conventional practice in the United States, feedlot cattle are given a diet of grains, which leads to quick weight gain and a higher percentage of fat. Several studies have indicated that grain, once introduced into cattle's diet, changes the health of their digestive tract (which is one of the reasons grain-fed cattle require antibiotics) and ultimately changes the composition of the meat.

When It Comes to Poultry, How Do I Know Which Label to Trust? Organic, Natural, Free-Range—What Does It Mean?

FREE-RANGE: In order to be labeled "free-range," chickens must have access to the outdoors for at least some part of the day, whether the chickens choose to go outside or not. Realistically, most chickens stay close to water and feed, which is usually located within the chicken house.

NATURAL: One of the most misleading marketing claims in the entire food world (which, if you think about it, is a most dubious distinction), under USDA regulations, a "natural" product has no artificial ingredients, coloring, or chemical preservatives and is minimally processed, just enough to get it ready to be cooked. Note that this has absolutely nothing to do with how the bird was raised, simply that nothing has been added after slaughter. Approach with skepticism! Remember, though, that "natural" in Canada refers to "naturally raised"—a whole different (and much healthier) animal.

ORGANIC: The USDA strictly governs the organic certification, and for chicken, it means that 100 percent of its feed must be certified organic. This means that the feed has to have been grown in a field that has not seen chemical fertilizers, fungicides, herbicides, or genetically modified organisms for at least three years. In addition to the feed regulations, certain techniques are prohibited in organic production. Since antibiotics are not allowed at all, chickens can't be contained in the tight confines that conventional producers use. By law, organic chickens must be free-range.

In Canada, chicken that is sold as "organic" is raised to a specific standard as laid out by the Canadian General Standards Board, in addition to the regulations set by a reputable organic certification board. Since these boards vary from province to province, there are slight differences in the rules for organic farming in different areas of the country. In general, organic chicken must be raised with certified organic feed that contains no animal by-products or antibiotics, and any supplements, such as vitamins, must be approved by a certification body.

RAISED WITHOUT HORMONES OR ANTIBIOTICS: Despite what you may have heard, no artificial or added hormones are used in the production of any poultry in the United States or Canada. Regulations of the Food and Drug Administration and the Canadian Food Inspection Agency prohibit such use. The words "raised without antibiotics" on a package of chicken indicate that the flock was raised without the use of products classified as antibiotics for animal health maintenance, disease prevention, or the treatment of disease. "Antibiotic-free" is not allowed to be used on a label but may be found in marketing materials not regulated by the U.S. Department of Agriculture. All chicken is "antibiotic-free" in the sense that no antibiotic residues are present in the meat at the time of purchase, as the government requires chicken producers to follow withdrawal periods and other precautions before poultry is sold; however, most conventionally raised chickens have antibiotics added to their feed.

PASTURED: A pastured bird is kept in a coop at night but left to forage on grass during the day. They might be fed grain as well, but they have

access to a greater variety of food in their diet. This often means their meat and eggs are much more richly flavored, and that the birds themselves lived a pretty nice life before going to slaughter. It's also much more expensive to raise chickens this way, because of the amount of space required and how that limits the number of chickens that can be raised at a time.

Beef, Wild Game, and Lamb

High in protein and iron, beef, lamb, and wild game like bison are great for babies. Iron is critical at the early stages of baby's development, so try to integrate as much of it as possible into baby's first bites. Look for grass-fed, grass-finished meat that has been raised without antibiotics or added hormones for the highest quality.

HOW TO BUY AND STORE: When selecting meat for preparation, choose a cut that is mostly lean. Wild game is leanest, but for baby, I suggest a cut that has light marbling, as a bit of fat makes the meat more tender. Some cuts of beef that work well for baby food are eye of round roast, top sirloin, and lean fresh ground. Store fresh cuts in the refrigerator for up to three days or in the freezer for up to six months.

HOW TO USE: Cook beef and wild game by roasting or steaming. This helps retain the most nutrients. Making a stew is the best way to tenderize meat, and a good stew incorporates a variety of vegetables, making a pureed cupful the most balanced baby meal you can offer.

Poultry

Chicken and turkey are excellent sources of protein and very good sources of niacin, phosphorus, vitamin B_6, and selenium. They are high in iron but low in saturated fats compared to other meats. Lean and mild in flavor, poultry is a wonderful first food. Babies tend to like the darker cuts of poultry because of the tender texture, so feed away, as darker poultry also has more iron.

HOW TO BUY AND STORE: I strongly recommend buying and serving organic or free-range chicken, free from steroids, hormones, and antibiotics. Aside from the health benefits of avoiding hormones and antibiotics, organic chicken tastes better, too. Buy chicken with opaque, spotless skin. If buying frozen, look to see if there is any frozen liquid in the packaging, as this could indicate the chicken thawed and then froze again, making it potentially unsafe to eat. When purchasing fresh or frozen chicken, make sure that it spends the least time possible in your car. It's a good idea to use a cooler or insulated pack to transport poultry, and then transfer it first thing to the refrigerator or freezer when you get home.

HOW TO USE: Poultry can be prepared many ways: boiling, steaming, pan frying, and roasting. For first purees and self feeding, I would recommend boiling or steaming as the addition of water helps create a smoother puree and softer pieces. Pan frying or roasting provides more flavor and juicy tenderness as baby becomes more comfortable with texture.

A serious concern when feeding baby poultry is the risk of food poisoning. The improper handling and storage of chicken is one of the most common causes of food poisoning because of salmonella in the birds. Raw or undercooked flesh could transfer bacteria to baby, so proper food handling practices must be followed. Key tips:

- Wrap fresh chicken well before placing it in the refrigerator. Make sure that it cannot drip onto or touch any foods nearby (including the shelf below).
- Keep fresh chicken in the refrigerator for a maximum of two days.
- Thaw frozen chicken on a plate in the refrigerator, not on the counter at room temperature.
- When preparing chicken, keep it away from other foods to avoid cross-contamination.
- Use a plastic (not wooden) cutting board that's dedicated only for chicken.
- Be sure to wash the countertop, the cutting board, the utensils, and your hands thoroughly after cutting up chicken.
- Use a meat thermometer. A whole chicken should have an internal temperature of 180°F before eating. Chicken pieces containing a bone should have an internal temperature of 170°F, and boneless pieces should have an internal temperature of 160°F.

Eggs

"Egg" has basically become synonymous with "perfect protein"—and for good reason. It supplies all the essential amino acids, which are the building blocks for hormones, skin, tissues, and more. They are considered essential because the body cannot make them on its own—we have to get them from food. So eat your eggs, and don't leave out the yolk! The yolk contains the choline, which plays a role in brain development and is important for memory storage, as well as protein and antioxidants. Note that Canada's new infant feeding guidelines state that babies can eat both parts of the egg at six months old. Previously it was advised to introduce only the yolk at six months and wait for the white until after twelve months.

HOW TO BUY AND STORE: Pastured, organic, cage-free, all-natural, omega-3s—which eggs to choose? The quality of the yolk depends on the quality of the food consumed by the chicken that laid it. This is why organic or pasture-raised eggs are naturally the best choice when it comes to feeding your baby. The yolks are typically darker in hue, as a reflection of the dense nutrients and rich omega healthy fats. Your local farmers' market is the best place to find these little gems.

Eggs should not be stored in the refrigerator door, but in the main body of the refrigerator to ensure that they keep a consistent and cool temperature. Keep your eggs in their original carton, as this protects them and keeps them from absorbing the strong odors of other foods in your fridge through the thousands of tiny pores in their shells. Checking the "best before" date on the carton is also the easiest way to tell if your eggs are fresh. Another way to determine freshness is to place an egg in a glass of water: A fresh egg will sink, while an older egg will float.

Speaking of freshness, I found this interesting piece of information on the Egg Farmers of Ontario site: "Check the 'Best Before' date stamped on the carton. This date is about thirty-five days from the packaging date. It indicates the length of time the eggs will maintain their Grade A quality. If kept refrigerated, the eggs can be consumed a week or two after that date. However, they should be used in a thoroughly cooked dish (e.g., baked, hard-cooked, or scrambled) rather than soft-poached or fried." So while eggs don't go bad immediately after their "best before" date, they may no longer be Grade A quality.

HOW TO USE: A quick scramble, a cheese omelet, or a simple egg, hard-boiled and diced, makes for a healthy, super easy meal for baby. You can also add egg into cooked veggie and rice dishes or fry it up alongside grated cheese for a finger food snack. For a fluffier texture, I stir 1 teaspoon of milk into a whisked egg before cooking.

Fish

Fish are a great source of many nutrients, but their greatest benefit lies in their high content of omega-3 fatty acids, which help promote infant brain development as well as boost immunity and vision. DHA (docosahexaenoic acid) is an omega-3 fatty acid vital for brain and eye development. Salmon is by far the best source of DHA—the star of the omega-3 world (alongside caviar!).[5]

But almost all seafood contains omega-3s, so try to give your baby a variety of low-mercury fish. Some of the high-mercury fish to avoid are marlin, orange roughy, swordfish, and tuna. That said, canned light tuna is lower in mercury than albacore (aka white tuna) and a good way to offer the benefits of fish to your children. Seek wild-caught over farmed varieties whenever possible, since farm-raised fish are higher in contaminants like PCBs (polychlorinated biphenyls).[6]

HOW TO BUY AND STORE: When buying fish, look for a distinct skin color and, above all, a clean, fresh "sea smell." Fillets should be translucent with no sign of discoloration. Refrigerate fish as soon as possible after purchase—remember, it's highly perishable and must be kept cool. Fresh fish in good condition and properly stored should last a day or two after purchase. All fish can be successfully frozen. Fresh white fish can be frozen for a maximum of six months. Oil-rich fish is best if used within three months.

HOW TO USE: Blend cooked, flaked fish into pasta, rice, or mashed potatoes alongside your baby's favorite veggies. Alternatively, cook and puree fish with lemon, olive oil, and seasonings and combine with pureed veggies or spread on toast or crackers. Coat strips of fish with a breading mixture and bake into fingers for self-feeders.

Greek Yogurt

I prefer Greek yogurt to "regular" yogurt because of its thick, creamy texture and high protein content. Greek yogurt is strained more than its regular yogurt counterpart, which means that the whey (protein that those with dairy allergies may react to) and the lactose (sugar) content is far lower. Those with an allergy to whey protein still won't be able to consume Greek yogurt, but those with lactose intolerance might find it easier to digest. Greek yogurt can contain double the protein of regular yogurt as well.

HOW TO BUY AND STORE: Look for the plain variety with the highest fat content for baby, which is usually 4 percent in Greek yogurt. Avoid low-fat, sugar-free, or sweetened varieties, as baby needs the fat but does not need harmful low-calorie sweeteners or added sugars. When it comes to yogurt, keep it simple: Plain is best. You can always sweeten it with your own fruit puree if baby finds it too tart. Before you buy yogurt, check the "best before" date on the package and choose the product with the latest date. Refrigerate yogurt immediately after purchasing and store it on the colder shelves. Once the package is opened, eat the yogurt within three days.

HOW TO USE: Greek yogurt is delicious on its own or blended with fruits and veggies for a boost of protein. I use it whenever a texture needs to be smoothed out and creaminess is desired. I also add it in baking and smoothies and as a creamy topping for soups, cereals, and even desserts.

Kefir

I offer my kids a glass of kefir every morning alongside their breakfast. Kefir is a probiotic fermented milk drink made from kefir grains, which contain a large range of beneficial bacteria, yeasts, minerals, vitamins, amino acids, proteins, and enzymes, the most important among them being vitamin A, vitamin B_2, B_{12}, vitamin D, vitamin K, calcium, magnesium, and phosphorus. These probiotic cultures help strengthen immunity. Unlike many other dairy products that are indigestible and high in disaccharide sugar (lactose), kefir is an ideal probiotic drink for kids intolerant to lactose.

HOW TO BUY AND STORE: You can make kefir at home relatively easily, or you can purchase it from most grocery stores in the dairy aisle. Kefir is stored in the refrigerator and should be consumed prior to the expiration date printed on the bottle, regardless of whether it has been opened or not.

HOW TO USE: I suggest serving kefir blended in a smoothie, the same way you would use milk or a dairy alternative, for a boost of protein. It has a very tart, even sour taste, so it may not be palatable on its own. Blend a tablespoon into a favorite fruit puree and mix this combination into baby cereal for a complete meal. It also makes a good replacement for buttermilk when baking.

herbs and spices

For your kids to grow into healthy eaters, they need to experience and appreciate a wide variety of tastes. Introducing herbs, spices, and seasonings at a young age is key to expanding your baby's palate. Opening up a world of flavor for baby can be as simple as a pinch to fruit and vegetable purees or any combination meal. The trick is to ensure the introduction is very slight (a mini-pinch, even) to present the new flavors gently, and then be creative with your combinations. Besides the wonderful flavor profile of these highlighted herbs and spices, they also offer a huge array of healing properties that baby can benefit from.

DELICATE HERBS
Basil
Belonging to the mint family, basil has a sweet, earthy flavor and works wonderfully with a number of fruit and vegetable purees, such as nectarines, peaches, beets, tomatoes, and beef. Not only is it versatile, but basil also contains many nutrients for baby's development such as vitamin K, which is essential for blood clotting, as well as vitamin C, calcium, magnesium, potassium, and iron. It has been used for years as a calming aid for indigestion and could benefit a baby who suffers from reflux or gas.

Dill
Dill is a warming herb and a rich source of beta-carotene, iron, and potassium. It can "strengthen" the spleen, liver, and stomach organs. Babies tend to love its aniseed flavor. Finely chop dill and add it to eggs, mashed potatoes, beets, or fish dishes.

Mint
This refreshing herb has been used all over the world to settle stomachs and aid digestion. It may also fight off harmful bacteria and fungi. Mint can be added to many green vegetables to make delicious purees and soups or combined with many fruit purees to freshen up a dessert.

Cilantro
Cilantro (or coriander) is a powerful herb full of an array of phytonutrients and antioxidants. Research suggests it may help remove heavy metals from the body, making it a natural cleansing agent, plus it stimulates healthy digestion, relieves gas, and may even ward off salmonella bacteria. It is also a rich source of vitamin C, calcium, magnesium, potassium, and iron. Cilantro pairs nicely with beans, avocados, melons, chicken, fish, and eggs.

Parsley
The health benefits of parsley for babies include a good supply of vitamins, minerals, and antioxidants. It offers a remedy for digestive disorders and is high in vitamins B_1, B_2, C, and K, which work to strengthen baby's immune system. Parsley combines nicely with peas, tomatoes, and fish, beef, and chicken dishes.

HOW TO BUY AND STORE: Purchase delicate herbs such as basil, cilantro, parsley, dill, and mint in bunches from your local farmers' market or supermarket—they're readily available. Buy them fresh, and make sure they are bright green with springy stems. Delicate herbs are very sensitive to heat and cold, so keep them fresh by propping them in a vase of water on the countertop, like cut flowers. These herbs are best added at the end of the cooking process.

HARDY HERBS

Oregano

Popular in Mediterranean cooking, aromatic oregano is a natural antioxidant, and there is some evidence that it works toward lowering cholesterol and preventing intestinal parasitic infections. It's also known to be antibacterial and antiviral, which can help fight off colds, so use it generously in the winter. Try it finely chopped and added to savory squash, beef, tomato, or quinoa dishes.

Rosemary

This fragrant herb has been hailed for its medicinal properties since ancient times. Rosemary was traditionally used to help alleviate muscle pain, improve memory, and boost the immune and circulatory systems. Because rosemary can be almost twig-like, I recommend grinding the leaves prior to using for baby. Try ground rosemary in mashed roasted sweet potatoes or chicken, or bake it into teething biscuits.

Sage

Sweet and savory, sage can be a wonderful addition to your baby food. Besides its delicate flavor, sage can help with cognitive performance and memory. Try finely chopped or ground sage added to roasted squash, potato, and poultry dishes.

Thyme

Thyme has been used as a healing herb for hundreds of years and can help ease chest and respiratory problems as well as digestive issues. It has also been shown to have antimicrobial and antibacterial properties. Thyme's fragrance combines nicely with fish, poultry, and sweet root vegetables.

HOW TO BUY AND STORE: Less delicate herbs are purchased the same way as delicate herbs: bright, fresh, and fragrant. To store these fresh herbs, wrap them loosely with a paper towel and place them in a plastic bag in the refrigerator. Before cooking with these herbs, strip the leaves off the woody stems.

SPICES

Cumin

Cumin is another digestive aid that adds warmth and flavor to vegetable and meat dishes. It's thought the seeds also may have anticarcinogenic effects. Cumin is a rich source of iron and has antibacterial properties.

Cinnamon

Cinnamon supports good digestive health, and some research says it can even ward off bacteria. Smelling its warming scent has been said to boost brain function, and eating cinnamon can help regulate blood sugar in diabetics. You can find cinnamon ground or in whole sticks. Although ground cinnamon is most often used in baby food, I like to throw a stick in the pot when cooking grains and puddings to infuse them with flavor. Cinnamon adds a delicious spiciness to all kinds of fruit and root veggie purees, as well as rice and quinoa dishes.

Nutmeg

Known as a relaxing spice, nutmeg can help you sleep better, as well as ease sore tummies, aid in digestion, and lessen nausea. Like cinnamon, nutmeg makes an excellent addition to pumpkin, apples, yams, berries, chicken, pears, and rice dishes.

Cardamom

Exotic cardamom has been used in Ayurvedic medicine to treat many digestive problems. It may also help prevent and relieve cold and flu symptoms. It can be used to enhance both sweet and savory dishes, so try combining it with yogurt, apples, bananas, beef, carrots, poultry, ginger, lamb, pears, peas, sweet potatoes, and salmon. It can be purchased in pod or ground form. A little goes a long way, so be sure to use a tiny pinch.

Turmeric

You probably know turmeric as the spice that contributes the yellow color to many curries and Indian dishes. Recent studies have catapulted turmeric into the medical headlines, as it contains curcumin, a substance that may prove useful in the fight against cancer. Turmeric has anti-inflammatory benefits and may also function as an antioxidant and stimulate the immune system. It's related to ginger, but has a mild flavor.

HOW TO BUY AND STORE: Most of the flavor and aroma of spices comes from the oils in them, and these are quite volatile, so keeping your spices fresh is all about keeping these oils locked in. Tumeric can be purchased fresh or dried. Buy small quantities at a time, as large budget packs will go stale before you have time to use them. Spices don't have to be kept in the dark, but do avoid direct sunlight and store them in a cool, dry part of the kitchen. Heat and light break down the all-important oils and degrade the antioxidants. I would recommend buying your spices at a local spice merchant or ethnic market. These places pride themselves on quality, much like a farmers' market.

Ginger

A delicious warming spice, ginger has long been known to relieve nausea and soothe motion sickness. It is also good at helping the immune system fight off colds and flu. Both fresh and dried ginger are pretty potent, so use small amounts when adding to purees. Ginger tastes lovely with ancient grain dishes, coconut, pumpkin, yogurt, and pears. Be sure to peel it before using (peeling with a spoon is easiest). Fresh ginger will keep in the refrigerator for two to three weeks when loosely wrapped in paper towels, or you can pop it in the freezer, as it defrosts well. Note that ginger can be purchased dried and ground, or fresh.

Garlic

Everyone knows garlic is good for what ails you. It's been used for centuries to help beat common colds and flus and gastric difficulties. Raw garlic can be very strong for baby, so be sure to start with a very small amount. Dried garlic powder is less potent than fresh garlic. It can be roasted alongside your vegetables, sautéed with meats or vegetables, or simply sprinkle a touch of garlic powder on basic cooked pasta or prepared meals. To maintain its healing properties and flavor, fresh, just-picked garlic needs to be kept in the refrigerator and used within a week. Whole bulbs of store-bought garlic will keep for several months or more when stored at room temperature in a dry, dark place that has ample air circulation. Remember, though, that fresh garlic will begin to lose potency once you start removing cloves from the bulb. To avoid mold, do not refrigerate or store garlic in plastic bags.

SEASONAL PRODUCE

In our technology-saturated lives, everything is available to us all the time. We can order clothes from Europe at 2:00 a.m. and Skype with a friend in Asia. Physical location and time don't matter as much as they used to, which, while convenient for many things, can also be alienating. It's important to have a sense of place.

Selecting food within your local growing seasons connects you to the world around you in a way that most of our lives strives to avoid. Not only are local foods better for you and better for the environment, but the flavors are so rich and vibrant, you'll feel like you're getting away with something! Freshly harvested produce is so tender and flavorful, it requires very little preparation, and limited prep doesn't just mean less time in the kitchen—it also means more nutrients. We want to expose our little ones to the brightest, boldest flavors to orient their palates toward fresh, whole-

some foods. So why should you buy seasonal produce?

IT'S A PARTY IN YOUR MOUTH! Fresh, locally harvested foods have their full, whole flavors intact. When fruits and vegetables are picked prior to their peak and transported all around the world, they do not ripen as effectively as they would in their natural environment, which ultimately affects their texture and taste.

IT HAS AN ABUNDANCE OF NUTRITION. Produce starts to lose nutrients shortly after being picked, so if you buy out of season, you're likely purchasing items that were picked much earlier and lost nutrients

every step of the way. When produce is harvested early enough to endure a long-distance shipping experience, it's not going to have the full complement of nutrients it might have contained had it been left to ripen naturally. Also, transporting fruits and vegetables sometimes requires irradiation and preservatives to protect the produce.

IT'S ENVIRONMENTALLY FRIENDLY. When produce is grown during its natural season, it is more resilient to pests and disease so requires less soil and pest management. Locally grown also reduces transportation distances and therefore has less of a carbon footprint.

IT SUPPORTS YOUR LOCAL FARMERS! Your local, seasonal food is, by definition, grown by your local farmers. Keeping your money in your town's economy helps everyone there thrive, and knowing who grows your food and where it comes from is an important part of building community. Besides, visiting your local farmers' market is a great way to spend a couple hours with your family and introduce your little ones to fresh produce.[7] It can save you money. When buying in season, you'll find harvests are generally larger, which drives down costs.

What's in season in your community will depend on your location, since growing seasons vary across the nation. I have provided a general seasonal food guide below for reference. Please see notes for more specific resources.[8]

seasonality chart	WINTER	SPRING	SUMMER	FALL
Apples	•	•	•	•
Apricots			•	
Artichokes		•		•
Arugula		•		•
Asparagus		•		
Avocados			•	
Basil			•	
Beets	•	•		•
Bell Peppers			•	•
Blackberries			•	
Blueberries			•	
Boysenberries			•	
Broccoli	•			•
Brussel Sprouts	•			•

		WINTER	SPRING	SUMMER	FALL
	Cabbage	•			•
	Cantaloupes			•	
	Carrots	•	•	•	•
	Cauliflower	•			•
	Celery	•			•
	Celery Root				•
	Chard		•	•	•
	Cherries			•	
	Chickpeas			•	
	Cilantro			•	
	Corn			•	
	Cranberries				•
	Cucumbers			•	

		WINTER	SPRING	SUMMER	FALL
	Edamame				•
	Eggplant			•	•
	Escarole	•			•
	Fava Beans		•		
	Fennel	•	•		•
	Fiddleheads		•		
	Figs			•	•
	Garlic		•	•	•
	Grapefruit	•	•		
	Grapes			•	•
	Green Beans	•	•	•	•
	Green Onions	•	•	•	•
	Herbs	•		•	•
	Kale	•		•	•

	WINTER	SPRING	SUMMER	FALL
Kiwi	•	•		
Kohlrabi			•	•
Leeks	•	•	•	•
Lemongrass			•	•
Lemons	•	•		
Lettuce			•	•
Limes			•	•
Mandarins	•			
Mangoes			•	
Melons			•	
Mint		•		
Mushrooms				•
Navel Oranges		•		
Nectarines			•	

	WINTER	SPRING	SUMMER	FALL
Okra			•	•
Onions			•	•
Oranges		•		
Parsley		•		
Parsnips		•		•
Pea Greens		•		
Peaches			•	
Pears		•		•
Peas		•	•	
Persimmons	•			•
Plums			•	
Pomegranates				•
Pomelos		•		

		WINTER	SPRING	SUMMER	FALL
	Potatoes				•
	Pumpkins				•
	Radicchio	•		•	•
	Radishes		•	•	•
	Raspberries			•	
	Rhubarb		•	•	
	Rutabagas	•			•
	Scallions		•		
	Shallots			•	
	Spinach		•	•	•
	Spring Onions		•	•	
	Strawberries			•	

		WINTER	SPRING	SUMMER	FALL
	Summer Squash			•	
	Sweet Onions		•	•	
	Sweet Potatoes	•			•
	Tangerines	•			
	Tomatoes			•	•
	Turnips	•	•		•
	Watermelon			•	
	Winter Squash	•			•
	Zucchini			•	•

chapter 3

become a gourmet baby food maker

tools of the trade

Food processor

There are many different kinds of food processors to suit all manner of pureeing needs: a mini processor, a 4 to 12-cup food processor, a high-speed blender, a handheld immersion blender—it really is up to you and depends on how you plan on using yours. The mini was my favorite when I was making meals for my babies, as I could take a small portion from the family meal to make baby's dinner, while the handheld immersion blender works wonderfully with large pots of soup, as it allows you to puree directly in the pot. High-speed blenders are great for smoothies, soups, and other recipes with substantial liquid—otherwise the food gets caught in the blades at the bottom. For all other purees, I recommend a standard food processor, as it allows the most flexibility in crafting texture for your baby's food.

Heavy-bottomed pot with a lid and steamer insert

A kitchen staple, you'll use this to steam fruits and veggies, boil water, simmer stews, and cook delicious porridge.

Vegetable peeler

A peeler removes the thinnest layer of skin, preserving the majority of the flesh. A peeler is much more accurate than a knife and a key instrument for prepping most fruits and veggies.

Good knives

Whether it's a paring knife or chef's knife, a high-quality knife will make your life much easier.

Chopping, dicing, and mincing will become second nature after a few weeks on this baby food–making journey, so invest in something that cuts well.

Potato masher

Potato mashers create the perfect silky texture. When pureed, potatoes' starch is released, which can turn them into a thick, gooey paste. A masher adds texture to root vegetables and fluffiness to potatoes.

Fine mesh strainer

A strainer is useful for removing small seeds, bits, and lumps from purees and straining liquid from cooked veggies, legumes, and grains.

Storage containers

To help keep you organized, choose glass containers that you can freeze, reheat, store, and wash with ease.

BPA-free ice cube trays

These will be your best friend when making single-serve baby food cubes. The little portions can be easily removed, transferred to a large storage bag, and stored in the freezer for quick meals.

Ziploc freezer bags

Not just for the freezer, resealables are also great for refrigerated leftovers and dry goods in the pantry. Be sure to keep a permanent marker nearby to label the bags with contents and dates.

Parchment paper

This will keep anything from sticking to your baking pan. Keep a roll nearby at all times.

Baking sheet

Baking and roasting your fruits, vegetables, and proteins easily brings out the most delicious flavors in your ingredients.

Top 10 tips and tricks for baby food success:

1. **USE FRESH, SEASONAL INGREDIENTS.** Lush, ripe fruits and vegetables will give you the richest flavor, helping develop baby's palate and love for good food. If this isn't possible, find a good frozen organic alternative to keep on hand. (We love Stahlbush Island Farms.)

2. **MAKE FOODS YOU WOULD EAT YOURSELF.** Your baby is the most important person in the world to you—so why wouldn't you feed your baby the best? Most of these recipes I created because I would want to eat them myself. If I would eat them, then I feel much better about feeding them to my baby. Plus, you are going to make such quantities of these, I guarantee you will be eating the leftovers, too.

3. **TEXTURE IS EVERYTHING.** Baby may reject a food because of the texture, not the taste. There is a gradual introduction to texture, moving from stage one through stage four:

   STAGE ONE: smooth puree
   STAGE TWO: smooth puree with subtle texture (80 percent smooth, 20 percent textured)
   STAGE THREE: chunky (80 percent textured, 20 percent smooth)
   STAGE FOUR: whole foods

If one texture doesn't appeal to baby, try another with that same food. If a puree comes out too runny, stir or process in cooked rice, quinoa, oat flakes, or lentils as a great way to add thickness and texture.

If a meal comes out too thick, play with your liquid content and processing times to create the best texture for your baby. Adding water, cow's milk, breast milk, or formula to overly thick meals will thin them out and make them more palatable for baby.

There are two different processing techniques: Pureeing means using a food processor and letting it run until the food is completely pulverized into a smooth consistency. Pulsing means turning the food processor on and off (most processors have a pulse button) so that you break the food down bit by bit, creating your desired consistency. Pulsing is best for chunkier textures.

4. **A MINI FOOD PROCESSOR IS A MUST.** You can take a cup of your family meal and blend it with a few tablespoons of liquid to create your baby's meal in seconds, with no mess.

5. **MIX BABY'S FAVORITES WITH BABY'S DISLIKES.** If baby does not immediately embrace an ingredient, try mixing it with one of their favorite foods, then gradually reduce the amount of the favored food until they have developed a taste for the new one. One possible combination is to mix pear into broccoli until baby takes to broccoli on its own.

6. **BATCH FREEZE!** Most of these recipes are big enough to provide leftovers for you to freeze for quick and easy future meals. Freeze baby food in ice cube trays and toddler meals in muffin tins.

7. **AMP UP YOUR BABY'S FOOD WITH ADDED NUTRITION.** Constipation an issue? Stir in Baby Lax (page 98) to any of your recipes. Need a probiotic? Add kefir or yogurt. Short on healthy fats? Stir in avocado, coconut oil, or seed butter. Worried about brain and body development? Add our Super Seed Blend (page 106) to your baby food for essential protein, omega-3s, and fiber.

8. **FREEZE TEETHING BISCUITS.** Frozen biscuits and breadsticks will not only last longer, but they also do not break as easily and melt more slowly in baby's mouth. Many babies like the sensation of cold on their gums.

9. **TURN YOUR FAMILY MEAL INTO BABY'S MEAL.** Make your family dinner baby-friendly. You'll be surprised at how easily you can turn your roast chicken or lasagna into a deliciously warming meal for your little one.

10. **BE CREATIVE!** These recipes are meant to act as guidelines and can be altered depending on the ingredients you have on hand and your baby's preferences and intolerances. Swap out fruits and veggies depending on the season and what looks good. You never know what deliciousness you may stumble upon!

the essentials

You should always have these items on hand, as you will use them regularly:

PANTRY ESSENTIALS

Flour of choice: light spelt, whole wheat, unbleached all-purpose, or a gluten-free blend
Grains such as rolled oats, quinoa, millet, amaranth, and brown rice
Dried herbs and spices such as cinnamon, ginger, cardamom, basil, sage, and oregano
Maple syrup
Pasta: whole wheat, brown rice, and mini baby stars
Canned black beans and chickpeas
Lentils
Coconut milk
Coconut oil
Chicken broth
Nut butter
Seeds such as hemp and chia
Onions
Sweet potatoes
Garlic

REFRIGERATED ESSENTIALS

Fresh berries
Greens such as spinach, broccoli, and kale
Carrots
Peppers
Greek yogurt
Milk of choice
Cheeses such as cheddar and Parmesan
Butter
Eggs
Kefir

PANTRY AND COUNTERTOP ESSENTIALS

Fresh fruits and veggies such as apples, bananas, and avocados

key tips for baby food storage and handling

Batch cooking and freezing will be a lifesaver for you busy parents. No one wants to be cooking and cleaning baby food dishes every day, so the recipes in this book are large enough to make sure you'll have extra for freezing. Freeze purees in ice cube trays for baby-size portions you can bring out for future meals. You and your baby will love the array of flavors waiting in the freezer.

Once you have prepared your delicious food, you will want to ensure it is stored safely. Properly storing, thawing, and heating your baby food is necessary for it to remain free from harmful bacteria and safe for baby to eat.

STORING

After cooking, allow purees to cool thoroughly at room temperature or in the refrigerator.

Reserve one or two servings for baby's meal the following day and store in an airtight container in the back of the refrigerator.

To freeze the remaining puree, fill each mold of an ice cube tray (roughly two to three tablespoons of puree per cube), wrap the tray with plastic, and place in the freezer for two hours, or until firm.

Once firm, pop the cubes out and store them in a labeled, resealable, locking freezer bag. Be sure to note the date on the bag. There are many plastic baby food storage containers on the market. If you're going to get one, be sure to seek out something that is BPA-free. Also, avoid glass containers, as they crack in the cold. Homemade purees can be stored in the refrigerator for about three days and in the freezer for three months.

THAWING AND REHEATING

To avoid harmful bacteria, NEVER thaw baby food at room temperature.

Remove portions from the freezer the night before you intend to serve them, place them in a glass dish, and thaw in the refrigerator.

If you thaw in the microwave, do so in a glass dish, use the defrost setting, and stir often.

If reheating the meal in the microwave (after having thawed it in the fridge), cook it in ten-second intervals, stirring in between and checking the food for hot spots.

Always test the temperature of the food before serving it to avoid burning baby's sensitive mouth.

Baby food can also be reheated in a small saucepan or frying pan. Cook on medium to low heat to avoid burning.

Once meals have been thawed, DO NOT refreeze. They can be stored in the fridge for up to two days.

chapter 4

simple purees:
6 months+

HOW TO READ DIETARY ICONS ON THE RECIPES

 GLUTEN FREE DAIRY FREE EGG FREE VEGETARIAN VEGAN

And so we arrive at the world of solids. Amid the excitement and the endless options, where to begin? How do you even know if your baby is ready for their first taste of food? The guidelines in chapter one will help you determine baby's readiness, but roughly, look for these:

Interest in food: Does your baby eagerly watch you eat and seem excited to try for him/herself?

Trunk control: Can your baby sit up (with support is fine) and have enough control to lean forward and show you that they want more?

Head control: Obviously, your baby needs to be able to hold their own head up before eating solids. And can they turn their head to signal that they have had enough?

Less tongue thrusting: This extrusion reflex is for sucking and has served your baby well until now. Around six months, this starts to decrease so that food will stay in their mouth and not automatically be forced back out by baby's tongue.

If baby is around six months old, and you can answer yes to all of the above, head bravely into this new world. The good news is that starting solids is easy now, with far less rigid guidelines than in the past. Iron sources should take priority, like pureed meats (blended with higher proportions of fruits and veggies if baby won't accept them on their own), fortified infant cereal, legumes, or eggs. Then you can add in fruits and veggies, grains, and dairy, in no particular order. Other than the most highly allergenic foods (wheat, dairy, soy, egg, fish, shellfish, peanuts, and tree nuts), there is no need to wait three days before introducing each food. In fact, introducing a variety of foods early on may build your baby's tolerance to more allergenic foods, as well as cultivate baby's palate.

Offer your baby a small amount of purees once or twice a day to start. If they want more than a small amount, go ahead and feed them more. If they don't take to the spoon, you can offer a bit from your finger or a favorite toy, or just let your baby mush it around. Continue to offer solids, but if your baby is slow to accept, that's okay. Milk will still be their main source of nutrition until twelve months regardless.

Many of these recipes can be scaled to yield several servings so that you can batch freeze the leftovers for later use. That said, you may not want to make too many freezable servings of a single puree, as within a matter of days to weeks, baby will move to increased texture or even finger foods. If you do have extra purees left over, you can always use the fruits to flavor yogurt, oatmeal, or smoothies, and the veggie and meat purees can go into chili, soup, or pasta sauce.

apple puree

MAKES 2 CUPS (FOUR ½-CUP SERVINGS)

A classic staple in any baby's diet, steamed and pureed apples are not only delicious on their own, but also a perfect mixer for many variations of fruits, veggies, and proteins. Their texture and natural sweetness make apples a base for many combination recipes. I use Golden Delicious, Fuji, or Gala apples, avoiding overly acidic varieties like Granny Smith and Pink Lady.

4 apples, peeled, cored, and diced

ADD the apples and enough water to cover to a small saucepan and bring to a boil. Cover, reduce the heat, and simmer on low for 8 to 10 minutes, or until soft.

TRANSFER the apples to a food processor, then puree with ⅔ cup water until very smooth. Add more water in 1-tablespoon increments if necessary.

TIP: Add a pinch of cinnamon for a new flavor.

TIDBIT: Apples can ease tummy troubles like diarrhea and constipation and keep baby's digestive system working smoothly.

SUITABLE FOR FREEZING.

pear puree

MAKES 2 CUPS (FOUR ½-CUP SERVINGS)

Another classic staple in any baby's diet, pureed pears are the perfect accompaniment to many fruits and veggies because of their mild, sweet taste and smooth texture. Pears are packed with fiber, vitamin C, and potassium. For this recipe I suggest the Bosc, Bartlett, or Anjou varieties.

4 ripe pears, peeled, cored, and diced

ADD the pears and enough water to cover to a small saucepan and bring to a boil. Cover, reduce the heat, and simmer for 10 minutes, or until soft.

TRANSFER the pears to a blender and puree with ½ cup water until very smooth. Add more water in 1-tablespoon increments if necessary.

TIP: Try adding a pinch of pumpkin pie spice to give it a bit of a kick.

TIDBIT: Pears are among the least acidic fruits, making them an ideal first food and gentle enough for babies with acid reflux.

SUITABLE FOR FREEZING.

mango puree

MAKES ONE ½-CUP SERVING

1 ripe mango

USE a knife with serrated edges to slice the thickest part of the mango on either side, cutting as close as possible to the pit. Make three horizontal and three vertical cuts (down to the peel but not through it) in the flesh of the mango. Scoop the flesh out with a spoon.

PUREE the mango in a food processor or blender until smooth. Add breast milk, formula, or water as needed to reach the desired consistency.

FOR a chunkier mango puree, mash the mango with a fork or potato masher instead of pureeing it.

TIP: For new textures and flavors, try mixing mango with other fruits, veggies, poultry, oatmeal, or yogurt.

TIDBIT: Mangoes are low in fat and calories and very high in fiber, which can help aid baby's digestion.

SUITABLE FOR FREEZING.

avocado puree

MAKES ONE ½-CUP SERVING

Avocados are full of healthy fats and essential minerals and nutrients like potassium and folate. When mixed with other foods, avocados can help absorb fat-soluble vitamins (E, D, A, and K). With its smooth and creamy consistency, it truly is one of the most convenient foods to serve baby without cooking and with very little prep—simply open up a ripe avocado and spoon straight into baby's mouth.

1 ripe avocado

SLICE the avocado in half lengthwise and twist the two halves apart.

STORE the half with the pit remaining in the refrigerator (keeping the pit in the avocado helps prevent it from turning brown).

SCOOP the flesh out of the remaining half into a bowl and mash with a fork. Serve.

TIP: Mix with 1 tablespoon breast milk or formula for a thinner consistency.

TIDBIT: Avocados ripen more quickly when in the company of an apple or banana.

SUITABLE FOR FREEZING.
(but best served immediately)

roasted sweet potato puree

MAKES 2 CUPS (FOUR ½-CUP SERVINGS)

A classic single-ingredient puree, sweet potatoes mix well with everything. You'll be revisiting this one many a time.

> 2 large sweet potatoes, scrubbed and halved lengthwise

PREHEAT the oven to 400°F. Line a baking sheet with parchment paper.

ARRANGE the sweet potatoes on the prepared baking sheet.

ROAST until tender when pierced with a knife, 25 to 30 minutes.

LET cool slightly, then remove the flesh from the skin and place in a food processor with ½ cup water. Puree until smooth, adding more water in 1-tablespoon increments until a smooth consistency is reached.

SHORT on time? Alternative:

steamed sweet potato puree

PEEL and cube the sweet potatoes.

BRING water to a boil in a saucepan with a steamer insert. Reduce the heat to medium, add the sweet potatoes, cover, and steam for 12 to 15 minutes, until tender.

TRANSFER the sweet potatoes to a blender and puree until very smooth, adding the steaming liquid to thin out the consistency.

TIDBIT: Sweet potatoes are a dark orange vegetable, supplying plenty of vitamin A through beta-carotene, which contributes to healthy eyes and skin. Remember to offer your baby lots of veggie variety, though—too much beta-carotene can cause skin to take on a (temporary) golden hue!

SUITABLE FOR FREEZING.

broccoli puree

MAKES 3 CUPS (SIX ½-CUP SERVINGS)

Broccoli was the first solid food I introduced to my babies, and to this day, it's one of their favorite side dishes. Simple, steamed broccoli always gets eaten. I have no doubt it's because it was part of their diet from the very beginning, and they developed a love for it at that early age.

> 1 pound broccoli florets and peeled stems, cut into 1-inch pieces

BRING water to a boil in a saucepan with a steamer insert. Reduce the heat to medium, add the broccoli, cover, and steam for 8 to 10 minutes, until tender.

TRANSFER the broccoli to a blender and puree until very smooth, adding the steaming liquid to thin out the consistency.

TIP: Try adding mashed avocado for a creamier texture (see Creamy Broccoli Avocado recipe, page 93).

TIP: If you don't have a steamer, add the broccoli and 2 cups water to a small saucepan. Bring to a boil, cover, and reduce the heat. Simmer on low for 8 to 10 minutes. Add the broccoli and cooking water to the processor and puree. Add more water in 1-tablespoon increments if a thinner consistency is desired.

TIDBIT: Broccoli's unique flavor can help babies expand their taste for food. Babies are more likely to accept broccoli than older kids, so get it in early.

SUITABLE FOR FREEZING.

carrot puree

MAKES 2 CUPS (FOUR ½-CUP SERVINGS)

Full of beta-carotene, carrots make a nutritious and delicious first food—earthy and naturally sweet, with a desirable smooth texture.

> 4 large carrots, peeled and diced

BRING water to a boil in a saucepan with a steamer insert. Reduce the heat to medium, add the carrots, cover, and steam for 8 to 10 minutes, until tender.

TRANSFER the carrots to a blender and puree until very smooth, adding the steaming liquid to thin out the consistency.

TIP: If you don't have a steamer, add the carrots and 1 cup water to a small saucepan. Bring to a boil, cover, and reduce the heat. Simmer on low for 8 to 10 minutes. Add the carrots and cooking water to the processor and puree. Add more water in 1-tablespoon increments if a thinner consistency is desired.

TIDBIT: Carrots are an excellent source of beta-carotene, which turns into vitamin A in the body. Vitamin A aids your baby's eyes.

SUITABLE FOR FREEZING.

roasted butternut squash puree

MAKES 3 CUPS (SIX ½-CUP SERVINGS)

Whenever possible, I roast my veggies, as it's the best way to bring out their rich, sweet flavors. That said, I have also included a steamed alternative if time is of the essence.

1 medium butternut squash, halved and seeded

PREHEAT the oven to 400°F. Line a baking sheet or casserole dish with parchment paper.

ARRANGE the halves cut side down on the prepared baking sheet or casserole dish. Pour ½ cup water into the pan or dish.

ROAST the squash until tender when pierced with a knife, 35 to 40 minutes.

LET cool slightly, then remove the flesh from the skin and place in a food processor with ½ cup water. Puree until smooth, adding more water in 1-tablespoon increments until a smooth consistency is reached.

SHORT on time? Alternative:

steamed butternut squash puree

PEEL, seed, and dice the butternut squash into cubes.

STEAM for 12 to 15 minutes, until tender. Drain, reserving the cooking water.

PUREE the squash in a high-speed blender along with ½ cup cooking water. Add more water in 1-tablespoon increments until the desired consistency is reached.

TIDBIT: Squash is an excellent source of vitamins A and C and has a pleasing, creamy texture, making it a perfect first food.

TIP: Try adding a pinch of ground sage or nutmeg for a new flavor.

SUITABLE FOR FREEZING.

roasted beet puree

MAKES 2 CUPS (FOUR ½-CUP SERVINGS)

4 large beets, scrubbed and halved lengthwise

PREHEAT the oven to 400°F.

LINE a baking sheet with parchment paper.

ARRANGE the beets on the prepared baking sheet.

ROAST until tender when pierced with a knife, 25 to 30 minutes. Transfer the beets to a food processor and puree until smooth. Add water in 1-tablespoon increments if a smoother consistency is desired.

SHORT on time? Alternative:

steamed beet puree

PEEL and cube the beets. (Remember, they stain, so wearing rubber gloves may be a good idea!)

BRING water to a boil in a saucepan with a steamer insert. Reduce the heat to medium, add the beets, cover, and steam for 12 to 15 minutes, until tender.

TRANSFER the beets to a blender and puree until very smooth, adding the steaming liquid to thin out the consistency.

TIDBIT: Roasting beets enhances their natural sweetness and makes them extra baby-friendly. Just remember that eating beets can change the color of baby's urine, so don't be alarmed if you see a reddish tinge!

TIP: Try steaming the beet greens and pureeing them along with the roasted beets for added nutrition.

SUITABLE FOR FREEZING.

potato puree

MAKES 2 CUPS (FOUR ½-CUP SERVINGS)

Potato is a staple that can be eaten on its own or combined with one of the protein purees to create a creamier, more desirable texture for babies just starting out. When babies start showing interest in feeding themselves, mashed potatoes are a wonderful finger food—messy, but worth it!

> 1 pound (roughly 1 large) Russet potatoes, washed well and cut into 1-inch chunks

BRING water to a boil in a saucepan with a steamer insert. Reduce the heat to medium, add the potatoes, cover, and steam for 14 to 16 minutes, until tender.

TRANSFER the potatoes to a blender and puree until very smooth, adding the steaming liquid to thin out the consistency.

FOR a thicker consistency, mash steamed potatoes with a potato masher, along with the steaming liquid or milk.

TIP: Potato tastes great combined with other veggie and meat purees. Season with a little basil, oregano, or thyme, and you have a new, flavorful blend for baby to experience.

TIDBIT: The skin of a potato provides the majority of its fiber as well as its nutrients, so this is not one to peel. Just wash well and eat up.

SUITABLE FOR FREEZING.

parsnip puree

MAKES 2 CUPS (FOUR ½-CUP SERVINGS)

"The magical white carrot" was a story I made up for my kids while we were eating parsnip fries one night. I had them convinced that the parsnip was a magical vegetable, with powerful healthy properties. Yes, it was a fun little story, but not without an element of fact: This delicious root veggie is something special. Somewhat underrated and underused, parsnips offer a unique sweet flavor with a perfectly creamy pureed texture.

> 1 pound medium parsnips, peeled and cut into 1-inch chunks

BRING water to a boil in a saucepan with a steamer insert. Reduce the heat to medium, add the parsnips, cover, and steam for 15 to 18 minutes, until tender.

TRANSFER the parsnips to a blender and puree until very smooth, adding the steaming liquid to thin out the consistency.

TIDBIT: Parsnips bring a nutty and sweet flavor to baby food. They contain over 10 percent of baby's daily values for vitamin C, folate, and fiber.

SUITABLE FOR FREEZING.

pea puree

MAKES 2 CUPS (FOUR ½-CUP SERVINGS)

Mild peas are delicious alone or mixed with any number of other veggies. You can make this puree with fresh or frozen peas. When buying fresh peas in the spring, look for pods that are intact and have a bright green color. Avoid canned peas—they're filled with sodium.

> 2 cups fresh or frozen peas (if using fresh, remove the pods)

BRING water to a boil in a saucepan with a steamer insert. Reduce the heat to medium, add the peas, cover, and steam for 3 to 5 minutes, or until tender.

DRAIN the peas and rinse with cold water for 3 minutes to stop the cooking process. Transfer the peas to a blender and puree until very smooth, adding the steaming liquid to thin out the consistency.

FOR a chunkier pea puree, mash the peas with a potato masher instead of pureeing them. Peas have a soft shell, which baby may not like. To remove these, run the pea puree through a food mill, strainer, or sieve.

TIP: Try mixing pea puree with root veggies, yogurt, or rice for added texture and variety.

TIDBIT: Peas are a wonderful first "green" food, as they are nutritious, sweet, and high in protein. Did you know that one cup of peas contains more protein than a tablespoon of peanut butter?

SUITABLE FOR FREEZING.

green bean puree

MAKES 3 CUPS (SIX ½-CUP SERVINGS)

Rich in vitamin A and fiber, green beans are a nutritious addition to a baby's diet. You can make green bean puree from fresh or frozen beans. Frozen beans actually puree better, as fresh bean shells leave a much more fibrous texture. Avoid canned beans, as they're filled with sodium.

> 1 pound fresh or frozen beans (if using fresh, remove the ends)

BRING water to a boil in a saucepan with a steamer insert. Reduce the heat to medium, add the green beans, cover, and steam for 3 to 5 minutes, or until tender.

DRAIN the green beans and rinse with cold water for 3 minutes to stop the cooking process. Transfer the beans to a blender and puree until very smooth, adding the steaming liquid to thin out the consistency. Green beans are very fibrous, which makes it hard to get a smooth consistency. To remove the tough outer layer, run the bean puree through a food mill, strainer, or sieve.

TIP: Try mixing green bean puree with root veggies, fruit purees, baby cereals, yogurt, or rice for added texture and variety.

TIDBIT: It's recommended to eat one green and one orange vegetable daily, as these tend to be high sources of folate and vitamin A. The darker the color, the better!

SUITABLE FOR FREEZING.

broiled beef puree

MAKES 2 CUPS (FOUR ½-CUP SERVINGS)

Beef is a great source of protein, iron, and vitamin B. A lean-cut puree combined with a creamy vegetable puree makes an ideal meal for baby. Choosing organic and/or grass-fed beef adds extra healthy omega-3 fats.

1½ pounds top sirloin steak (1 inch thick)

BRING the beef to room temperature.

PREHEAT the broiler and line a rimmed baking sheet with foil.

PLACE the steak on the baking sheet and place under the broiler, about 4 inches from the heat source.

BROIL for 4 minutes, flip, and broil for another 4 minutes.

REMOVE from the oven and slice the center to make sure the steak is cooked through. If not, put the steak back for another couple of minutes and then check again.

TRANSFER the steak to a cutting board and let stand 1 minute.

COARSELY chop and transfer to a food processor or blender. Puree for 1 minute. Add water 1 tablespoon at a time until it has a smooth consistency.

TIP: As an alternative to broiling steak, if you have precooked beef of any cut, take 1 cup, ground or chopped, and process it until a powdery texture is formed, then add ¼ cup water so that a paste is formed. Add more liquid 1 tablespoon at a time until the desired consistency is reached.

TIP: My babies always pulled out the gag reflex when given a pureed protein like this one, so I always combined it in a 1:3 ratio of meat to pureed vegetables and fruit. The familiar, sweet taste of the veggies and fruit helped the protein go down more easily.

TIDBIT: It is important to introduce iron-rich foods like beef, as baby's iron reserves start to deplete at six months.

SUITABLE FOR FREEZING.

poached chicken puree

MAKES 1½ CUPS (THREE ½-CUP SERVINGS)

When introducing baby to proteins for the first time, texture is essential, as dry, chalky foods tend to be refused by these little critics. For this reason, I suggest poaching chicken to create the moistest and juiciest recipe possible. Serving chicken as a stand-alone meal may not go over well, so I recommend blending protein purees with a smooth pureed vegetable such as sweet potato, pumpkin, or parsnip.

½ pound boneless, skinless chicken breast

BUTTERFLY the chicken breast, slicing horizontally across, then opening up the two halves like a book.

IN a frying pan over medium heat, bring approximately ½ inch water to a simmer. Add the chicken breast; water should reach halfway up the sides of the chicken.

COOK, turning once, until the chicken is cooked through and no longer pink in the center, approximately 8 to 12 minutes.

TRANSFER the chicken to a cutting board, reserving the cooking liquid. Coarsely chop the cooked chicken and transfer to a blender or food processor along with 3 tablespoons cooking liquid. Puree on high until a smooth paste is achieved. If necessary, add more cooking liquid, 1 tablespoon at a time, if a smoother consistency is desired.

TIP: As an alternative to poaching, if you have pre-cooked boneless chicken, ground or chopped, take 1 cup and process it until powdery. Mix in ¼ cup water so that a paste is formed. Add more liquid 1 tablespoon at a time until the desired consistency is reached.

TIDBIT: High in protein and iron, chicken is the most recommended first meat for baby.

SUITABLE FOR FREEZING.

poached white fish puree

MAKES 2 CUPS (FOUR ½-CUP SERVINGS)

Fish is highly nutritious and an excellent source of protein, minerals, vitamins, and essential fatty acids. A white fleshy fish such as haddock, cod, sole, or flounder is a great choice for baby's first taste. The key is to ensure you have removed every single fish bone, as these can be a choking hazard.

1 pound boneless white fish

IN a medium saucepan, bring 2 cups of water to a boil. Reduce the heat to low, add the fish, cover, and poach for 7 to 10 minutes, until the fish is opaque and cooked through.

REMOVE the fish with a slotted spoon, reserving the poaching liquid. Transfer to a high-speed blender and puree, adding reserved poaching water 1 tablespoon at a time until a smooth, creamy texture is achieved.

TIP: Tastes yummy with potato puree, 1 teaspoon butter, and a pinch of dried herbs.

TIP: If you have precooked boneless fish in the fridge, process 1 cup fish with ¼ cup water until smooth. Add more liquid 1 tablespoon at a time until the desired consistency is reached.

TIP: Combine fish puree in a 1:3 ratio of fish to pureed vegetables and fruit, as babies sometimes find it hard to take proteins as they are. The greater proportion of sweeter, familiar purees will help them accept the fish.

TIDBIT: White fish is easily digestible and the perfect protein for baby's ongoing growth and development.

SUITABLE FOR FREEZING.

brown rice cereal

MAKES EIGHT ¼-CUP SERVINGS

½ cup organic short grain brown rice

PLACE brown rice in a high-speed blender or spice/coffee grinder for 50 to 60 seconds or until finely ground into a powder.

TO make 1 serving, bring ½ cup of water to a boil in a small pot, then add 2 tablespoons of ground rice, whisking continuously for 30 seconds.

COVER the pot and reduce the heat to low. To prevent lumps, stir occasionally for 5 minutes, until the mixture is thick and creamy. Allow to cool before serving.

TIP: To mix it up a bit, add baby's favorite puree or mash to prepared cereal. For added nutrition, try reducing the water to ¼ cup and add ¼ cup of breast milk.

TIDBIT: Where white rice has had the bran and germ removed, brown rice lacks only the hull, so it retains more of its nutritional value.

Store extra ground rice in a sealed container in a cool, dark place.

millet cereal

MAKES EIGHT ¼-CUP SERVINGS

Millet is a super healthy whole grain and a great first cereal. Like rice, it is not likely to cause allergies and is easily digested.

½ cup organic millet

PLACE millet in a high-speed blender or spice/coffee grinder for 20 to 30 seconds or until finely ground into a powder.

TO make 1 serving, bring ½ cup of water to a boil, then add 2 tablespoons of ground millet, whisking continuously for 30 seconds.

COVER the pot and reduce the heat to low. To prevent lumps, stir occasionally for 5 minutes, until the mixture is thick and creamy. Allow to cool before serving.

STORE extra ground millet in a sealed container in a cool, dark place.

TIP: For meal variety, add baby's favorite puree or mash to prepared cereal. For added nutrition, try reducing the water to ¼ cup and add ¼ cup of breast milk.

TIDBIT: Millet contains a good amount of fiber, which means more regularity and better digestion for your little one.

oatmeal cereal

MAKES EIGHT ¼-CUP SERVINGS

½ cup old-fashioned rolled oats

PLACE oats in a high-speed blender or spice/coffee grinder for 20 to 30 seconds or until finely ground into a powder.

TO make 1 serving, bring ½ cup of water to a boil, then add 2 tablespoons of ground oatmeal.

WHISK continuously for 30 seconds and then occasionally for 3 to 5 minutes, until the mixture is thick and creamy. Allow to cool before serving.

STORE leftover oat powder in a sealed container in a cool, dark place for up to 3 months.

TIP: For meal variety, add baby's favorite puree or mash to prepared cereal. For added nutrition, try reducing the water to ¼ cup and add ¼ cup of breast milk.

TIDBIT: Oats are a great first cereal for your baby, chock-full of vitamins, minerals, fiber, and protein.

Use certified gluten-free oats if your baby is sensitive to gluten.

amaranth cereal

MAKES EIGHT ¼-CUP SERVINGS

½ cup amaranth

PLACE amaranth in a high-speed blender or spice/coffee grinder for 20 to 30 seconds or until finely ground into a powder.

TO make 1 serving, bring ½ cup of water to a boil in a small pot, then add 2 tablespoons of ground amaranth, whisking continuously for 30 seconds.

COVER the pot and reduce the heat to low. To prevent lumps, stir occasionally for 5 minutes, until the mixture is thick and creamy. Allow to cool before serving.

STORE extra ground amaranth in a sealed container in a cool, dark place.

TIP: To mix it up a bit, add baby's favorite puree or mash to prepared cereal. For added nutrition, try reducing the water to ¼ cup and add ¼ cup of breast milk.

TIDBIT: Amaranth contains a decent amount of lysine, an amino acid often missing from the plant kingdom, making it closer to a complete protein than any other grain.

quinoa cereal

MAKES EIGHT ¼-CUP SERVINGS

½ cup quinoa

PLACE quinoa in a high-speed blender or spice/coffee grinder for 20 to 30 seconds or until finely ground into a powder.

TO make 1 serving, bring ½ cup water to a boil in a small pot, then add 2 tablespoons of ground quinoa, whisking continuously for 30 seconds.

COVER the pot and reduce the heat to low. To prevent lumps, stir occasionally for 5 minutes, until the mixture is thick and creamy.

TIP: To mix things up a bit, add baby's favorite puree or mash to prepared cereal. For added nutrition, try reducing the water to ¼ cup and add ¼ cup of breast milk.

TIDBIT: Quinoa does not contain gluten, so it's ideal for babies who can't consume wheat.

Store extra ground quinoa in a sealed container in a cool, dark place.

barley cereal

MAKES EIGHT ¼-CUP SERVINGS

½ cup barley

PLACE barley in a high-speed blender or spice/coffee grinder for 50 to 60 seconds or until finely ground into a powder.

TO make 1 serving, bring ½ cup of water to a boil in a small pot, then add 2 tablespoons of ground barley, whisking continuously for 30 seconds.

COVER the pot and reduce the heat to low. To prevent lumps, stir occasionally for 5 minutes, until the mixture is thick and creamy. Allow to cool before serving.

TIP: Add prepared cereal to baby's favorite puree or mash to give meals a bit of variety. For added nutrition, try reducing the water to ¼ cup and add ¼ cup of breast milk.

TIDBIT: Eating barley is believed to help regulate blood sugar and lower cholesterol, as well as prevent heart disease and certain types of cancer.

Store extra ground barley in a sealed container in the refrigerator.

chapter 5
creative combos:
6 months+

These recipes introduce baby to a wider array of flavors, as we start to integrate herbs and spices. Offering a variety of taste experiences now will expand baby's palate, so that your child may be more likely to grow into an adventurous eater as they get older. Anything from mint (try Minty Green Pea and Barley Puree, page 107) and ginger (Carrot Apple Ginger, page 98) to cinnamon and nutmeg (Spiced Apples, Figs, and Spinach Amaranth, page 104) are good choices—just avoid adding salt and sugar.

At this stage, it is important to include less liquid and not blend these purees quite so smoothly, as you want baby to start to accept different consistencies. Failing to offer more texture before nine months may make it more difficult for baby to learn how to deal with lumps and bumps in their food. Yes, some babies have a more sensitive gag reflex and will gag as you progress to chunkier foods. This is okay! Don't overreact and scare your baby.

Gagging is a normal part of learning how to eat solids; they are just bringing the food back up to chew it some more. Of course, it's important to always watch your baby while they eat, and don't offer round items (like whole grapes, cherries, hot dogs, or popcorn) that could pose real choking hazards.

Continue to offer your baby iron at each meal, whether it be from infant cereal, beans, a scrambled egg, or a recipe that includes meat, like Root Veggies and Beef (page 108). Beyond that, you can introduce all foods at six months, except for honey (because of the botulism risk) and fluid milk. You should wait until nine to twelve months to make fluid cow's milk your baby's main milk source, as it lacks the iron and nutrients in breast milk or formula.

juicy pears and garden greens

MAKES 1 CUP (TWO ½-CUP SERVINGS)

JPGG, as it's known to the team at Baby Gourmet, has been our number-one seller, year after year. It's a delicious way to introduce your little one to greens.

> 1 cup water
> 2 ripe pears, peeled, cored, and diced
> ½ broccoli floret, washed and chopped (stems peeled)
> 1 handful fresh spinach, washed

ADD the water to a small saucepan and bring to a boil. Add the pears, broccoli, and spinach. Cover, reduce the heat, and simmer for 10 minutes or until fork-soft.

TRANSFER the pears, broccoli, spinach, and cooking water to a blender, then puree until very smooth. Add more water in 1-tablespoon increments if necessary.

TIP: Try blending in pureed white fish or chicken for added protein.

TIDBIT: Pears are one of the richest suppliers of antioxidants. High in fiber, potassium, and vitamin C, they can also alleviate baby's constipation.

TIDBIT: Spinach contains calcium and magnesium, which are essential for baby's bone development.

SUITABLE FOR FREEZING.

apple raspberry

MAKES 2 CUPS (FOUR ½-CUP SERVINGS)

> 4 apples, peeled, cored, and diced
> ⅔ cup water
> ½ cup raspberries

ADD the apples and water to a small saucepan and bring to a boil. Add the raspberries, cover, reduce the heat, and simmer on low for 8 to 10 minutes, or until soft.

TRANSFER the apples, berries, and cooking water to a food processor; puree until very smooth. Add more water in 1-tablespoon increments if necessary.

TIP: Add a pinch of dried mint for a new flavor.

TIDBIT: The tiny seeds in raspberries are a great source of dietary fiber.

SUITABLE FOR FREEZING.

pear pumpkin banana

MAKES 2 CUPS (FOUR ½-CUP SERVINGS)

A popular, classic Baby Gourmet recipe, your little ones are sure to love the way the richness of the pumpkin is balanced by the sweetness of the pear and banana.

> 2 ripe pears, peeled, cored, and chopped
> ½ cup water
> ½ cup canned pumpkin
> 1 ripe banana, peeled

ADD the pears and water to a small saucepan and bring to a boil. Cover, reduce the heat, and simmer for 10 minutes, or until fork-soft.

TRANSFER the pears, cooking water, pumpkin, and banana to a food processor, then puree until very smooth. Add more water in 1-tablespoon increments if a thinner consistency is desired.

TIP: Try blending in plain Greek yogurt or tofu puree for added protein.

TIDBIT: When people talk about pumpkins, they tend to talk about their taste, but pumpkins are also full of nutrients like calcium, magnesium, iron, and vitamins C and A—all of which support baby's development.

SUITABLE FOR FREEZING.

fennel and apples

MAKES 2 CUPS (FOUR ½-CUP SERVINGS)

> 1 small fennel bulb (white part only), trimmed and chopped
> 2 apples, peeled, cored, and chopped
> 1 cup water
> Pinch of cinnamon (optional)

PLACE the fennel, apples, and water in a small saucepan. Bring to a boil, cover, reduce the heat, and simmer on low for 10 minutes, or until the fennel is fork-tender.

TRANSFER the fennel, apples, cooking water, and cinnamon (if using) to a food processor and puree until smooth. Add more water in 1-tablespoon increments if a thinner consistency is desired.

TIP: Make it a more complete meal by adding 1 tablespoon pureed cooked chicken or turkey or 2 tablespoons hemp hearts to each ½-cup portion for added protein and nutrition.

TIDBIT: Fennel, with the delicious essence of anise, is a wonderful natural remedy to ease gas and digestion for baby.

SUITABLE FOR FREEZING.

creamy broccoli avocado

MAKES 2 CUPS (FOUR ½-CUP SERVINGS)

Broccoli puree on its own can have a texture and flavor that some babies may not take to immediately, so I added avocado to smooth out the texture and soften the flavors. The outcome is a deliciously creamy superfood puree that baby will devour!

> ½ pound broccoli florets and peeled stems, cut into 1-inch pieces
> 1 ripe avocado, peeled and pitted

BRING water to a boil in a saucepan with a steamer insert. Reduce the heat to medium, add the broccoli, cover, and steam for 8 to 10 minutes, until tender.

TRANSFER the broccoli to a blender, add the avocado, and puree until very smooth, adding the steaming liquid to thin out the consistency.

TIP: If you don't have a steamer, add the broccoli and 1 cup water to a small saucepan. Bring to a boil, then cover and reduce the heat. Simmer on low for 8 to 10 minutes. Put the cooked broccoli, all the cooking water, and the avocado into a food processor and puree until smooth. Add more water in 1-tablespoon increments if a thinner consistency is desired.

TIP: To prevent browning of the avocado, stir a few drops of lemon juice into the puree prior to storage.

TIDBIT: Did you know an avocado has more potassium than a banana? A single avocado has 975 milligrams of potassium, while a banana, well-known for being loaded with potassium, delivers just half that, with 487 milligrams per large fruit.

SUITABLE FOR FREEZING.

baby's first chia pudding

MAKES ONE ½-CUP SERVING

I am a huge fan of chia seeds and believe their powerhouse nutritional benefits should be introduced to baby early. This is a simple starter pudding your little ones will love.

> ½ cup applesauce
> 1 tablespoon water
> 1 tablespoon chia seeds

COMBINE all the ingredients and stir until well combined. Allow to sit for 10 minutes before serving. Place in a resealable container, cover, and refrigerate.

TIP: Chia absorbs liquid and thickens over time. If your pudding ends up too thick, add water in 1-tablespoon increments to thin out the consistency.

TIP: You can substitute the applesauce with another fruit puree of your choice.

TIDBIT: Chia is packed with omega-3 fatty acids, which are important for a baby's brain development.

super fruity greens

MAKES 2 CUPS (FOUR ½-CUP SERVINGS)

> ½ cup water
> 2 apples, peeled, cored, and diced
> ½ cup chopped kale
> ½ cup spinach, chopped
> 1 large banana

ADD the water to a small saucepan and bring to a boil. Add the apples, kale, and spinach. Cover, reduce the heat, and simmer for 10 minutes, or until soft.

TRANSFER the apples, greens, and cooking water to a blender; add the banana and puree until very smooth. Add more water in 1-tablespoon increments if necessary.

TIP: Try mixing in the Super Seed Blend (page 106) for added nutrients.

TIDBIT: Bananas are so much more than just a sweet treat for baby. They contain potassium, fiber, and vitamins B and C.

TIDBIT: Spinach delivers lots of calcium and magnesium, which are essential for baby's bone development.

SUITABLE FOR FREEZING.

apple sweet potato berry swirl

MAKES 2 CUPS (FOUR ½-CUP SERVINGS)

Another popular recipe from the Calgary Farmers' Market, this delicious blend of creamy sweet potatoes, apples, and mixed berries will tantalize baby's taste buds.

    1 large sweet potato, peeled and diced
    ½ cup water
    2 apples, peeled, cored, and diced
    ¼ cup blueberries, fresh or frozen
    ¼ cup raspberries, fresh or frozen

PLACE the sweet potatoes in a saucepan with the water. Bring to a boil, cover, reduce the heat, and simmer on low for 10 minutes.

AFTER 10 minutes, add the apples, blueberries, and raspberries, continuing to simmer for an additional 10 minutes, or until fork-soft.

TRANSFER the sweet potatoes, apples, berries, and cooking water to a blender; puree until very smooth. Add more water in 1-tablespoon increments if necessary.

TIDBIT: "An apple a day" works for baby, too. Apple puree is easy to digest, and its soluble fiber helps fight against constipation.

SUITABLE FOR FREEZING.

roasted beets and apple millet

MAKES 4 CUPS (EIGHT ½-CUP SERVINGS)

3 large beets, scrubbed and halved lengthwise
3 medium apples, cored and halved lengthwise (skin on)
1 tablespoon olive oil
½ teaspoon cinnamon
½ cup cooked millet

PREHEAT the oven to 400°F. Line a baking sheet with parchment paper.

ARRANGE the beets and apples on the prepared baking sheet. Drizzle with the olive oil and sprinkle with cinnamon.

ROAST until tender when pierced with a knife, 25 to 30 minutes.

TRANSFER the beets, apples, and millet to a food processor and puree until smooth. Add water in 1-tablespoon increments if a smoother consistency is desired.

IF more texture is desired, do not add the millet to the processor—simply stir it into the mixture before serving.

TIDBIT: Eating beets can give baby's urine a pink or red tinge, so don't be alarmed if you notice an unusual hue.

TIDBIT: Millet acts as a probiotic to feed important microflora in baby's digestive system.

TIDBIT: If your baby's a little grouchy, beets may be just the thing! They contain betaine, which is known to improve mood.

SUITABLE FOR FREEZING.

baby lax

MAKES 1½ CUPS (TWENTY-FOUR 1-TABLESPOON SERVINGS)

One of the top complaints among moms when introducing solids is baby constipation. Jill created this recipe to serve on its own or mixed up with baby cereal to help ease baby's pain.

  ½ cup raisins
  ¼ cup prunes
  4 large dried figs
  6 tablespoons prune juice
  ¼ cup natural bran
  ¼ ripe pear, peeled and cored

SOAK the dried fruit in hot water for up to an hour, until soft.

DRAIN and then combine all the ingredients in a food processor until the consistency is smooth. Cover and refrigerate or freeze unused portions.

TIP: Try blending with baby cereal or a favorite fruit or veg puree.

TIDBIT: Figs contain dietary fiber and have been used for centuries as a natural laxative. Giving figs to your baby regularly will help constipation.

SUITABLE FOR FREEZING.

carrot apple ginger

MAKES 2 CUPS (FOUR ½-CUP SERVINGS)

Inspired by the recipe for one of my favorite juices, I took a chance that my baby might like the powerful flavor of ginger. Ginger is known to help with digestion and to ease tummy aches. When I realized my daughter had something of a sensitive tummy, I wanted to give her ginger and see if it helped. She loved this combination, and so did many of the babies in my mommy group.

  2 large carrots, peeled and sliced
  1 cup water
  3 apples, peeled, cored, and diced
  1 teaspoon fresh ginger, peeled and grated

PLACE the carrots and water in a small saucepan. Bring to a boil, and then add the apples and ginger. Reduce the heat, cover, and simmer for 10 minutes, or until fork-soft.

TRANSFER the carrots, apples, ginger, and cooking water to a food processor and puree until smooth. Add more water in 1-tablespoon increments if necessary.

TIP: Try adding ½ teaspoon tahini (ground sesame seeds) to a ½-cup portion for added nutrition and a variation in flavor.

TIDBIT: Small amounts of ginger can help with baby's digestive issues.

SUITABLE FOR FREEZING.

cardamom parsnip pear

MAKES 3 CUPS (SIX ½-CUP SERVINGS)

2 large parsnips, peeled and sliced
1 cup water
2 pears, peeled, cored, and chopped
1 leek, white part only, washed, trimmed, and sliced
1 cup milk, water, or vegetable stock
½ teaspoon ground cardamom

PLACE the parsnips and water in a small saucepan and bring to a boil. Reduce the heat, add the pears, and simmer on low for 10 minutes, or until fork-tender.

TRANSFER the parsnips, pears, and cooking liquid to a food processor. Add the milk and carda-mom and blend until smooth. Add more milk in 1-tablespoon increments if a thinner consistency is desired.

TIP: Make it a more complete meal by adding 1 table-spoon pureed cooked chicken or silken tofu to every ½-cup portion. Or try adding ¼ cup hemp hearts to the saucepan during the simmering stage for added nutrition.

TIDBIT: Parsnips are a good source of folate, which is critical for brain health. Beyond reducing the risk of neural tube defects in pregnancy, folate may be linked to the prevention of strokes and depression in adulthood.

Can be made dairy-free by substituting water or vegetable stock for the milk

SUITABLE FOR FREEZING.

black bean banana lime mash

MAKES 2 CUPS (FOUR ½-CUP SERVINGS)

One (15-ounce) can black beans
2 small ripe bananas
2 teaspoons fresh lime juice

RINSE the black beans under cold water to remove the canning liquid and excess sodium.

PLACE the beans, bananas, and lime juice in a food processor with 3 tablespoons breast milk, water, or formula and puree, adding more liquid in 1-tablespoon increments until the desired consistency is reached.

TIP: Try a pinch of cilantro for a new flavor.

TIDBIT: The darker the beans, the more antioxidants they contain, so black beans are chock-full!

SUITABLE FOR FREEZING.

gingered tahini carrots and parsnips

MAKES 2 CUPS (FOUR ½-CUP SERVINGS)

2 large carrots, peeled and sliced
1 large parsnip, peeled and sliced
2 slices (¼-inch-thick) fresh ginger, peeled
1 tablespoon maple syrup
½ teaspoon tahini (sesame seed paste)

IN a medium saucepan, combine the carrots, parsnips, ginger, and maple syrup. Add enough water to cover by 1 inch and bring to a boil. Reduce the heat to a simmer, cover, and cook until the vegetables are tender, about 10 minutes.

RESERVE 1 cup of the cooking liquid, then drain. In a food processor, combine the vegetables and tahini with ¼ cup cooking liquid and puree until a smooth consistency is reached. If a thinner consistency is desired, add more cooking water in 1-tablespoon increments.

TIP: Try adding 1 tablespoon cooked rice to a ½-cup serving for texture or 1 tablespoon baby cereal for added iron.

TIDBIT: Did you know that tahini is one of the best sources of calcium? Just 2½ tablespoons of tahini contain almost 16 percent of your recommended daily calcium intake. It's also high in healthy, unsaturated fats.

SUITABLE FOR FREEZING.

peachy coconut tofu

MAKES 2 CUPS (FOUR ½-CUP SERVINGS)

You have to love a protein-packed meal that requires no cooking! This recipe couldn't be easier, and babies can't get enough of the flavor combination.

> 2 large ripe peaches, peeled and cubed
> 1 cup cubed silken tofu*
> 3 tablespoons coconut milk

IN a high-speed blender, combine all the ingredients and blend until smooth.

ADD more coconut milk in 1-tablespoon increments if a thinner consistency is desired.

TIP: Try substituting banana, nectarine, or mango for the ripe peach. Maybe add a pinch of fresh mint as well!

TIDBIT: Tofu is a very versatile ingredient, taking on the flavor of whatever you pair it with. It's a great source of protein, B vitamins, iron, and calcium, all essential building blocks for baby's health.

It's important to buy organic tofu, as soybeans are one of the largest genetically modified crops.

banana chia pudding

MAKES 2 CUPS (FOUR ½-CUP SERVINGS)

> 2 bananas
> 1 cup water
> 3 tablespoons chia seeds

IN a high-speed blender, combine the bananas and water, blending until smooth.

POUR the banana puree into a bowl with the chia seeds. Whisk until blended.

PLACE in a resealable container, cover, and refrigerate.

TIP: Chia swells in liquid and thickens over time. If the pudding is too thick, add water in 1-tablespoon increments to thin out the consistency.

TIP: To prevent browning, stir in a few drops of lemon juice before storage.

TIDBIT: Bananas are the perfect portable baby food, as they come in their own easy-to-peel packaging.

roasted sweet potato parsnip coconut mash

MAKES 2½ CUPS (FIVE ½-CUP SERVINGS)

This creamy mash is super yummy on its own, as a side dish for your next turkey dinner, or as a topping for your favorite chicken pie recipe.

> 1 pound sweet potatoes, peeled and cut into ½-inch cubes
> ½ pound parsnips, peeled and sliced
> 1 tablespoon olive oil
> ½ teaspoon ground sage
> ¾ cup coconut milk

PREHEAT the oven to 400°F. Line a baking sheet with parchment paper.

TOSS the sweet potatoes and parsnips with the olive oil and sage. Arrange in a single layer on the prepared baking sheet.

ROAST the vegetables until tender when pierced with a knife, 25 to 30 minutes.

IN a food processor, pulse all the ingredients together, along with the coconut milk. Add more coconut milk in 1-tablespoon increments until the desired consistency is reached.

TIP: Make it a more complete meal by adding 1 tablespoon pureed cooked chicken or pork to a ½-cup portion for added protein.

TIDBIT: Coconuts contain lauric acid, which is found in breast milk. Lauric acid protects the body from infections and helps boost the immune system.

SUITABLE FOR FREEZING.

spiced apples, figs, and spinach amaranth

MAKES 4 CUPS (EIGHT ½-CUP SERVINGS)

3 medium apples, cored and halved lengthwise (keep the peel on)

3 large fresh figs, halved lengthwise

1 tablespoon maple syrup (optional)

½ teaspoon cinnamon

½ teaspoon nutmeg

2 cups fresh spinach

½ cup cooked amaranth

PREHEAT the oven to 400°F. Line a baking sheet with parchment paper.

ARRANGE the apples and figs on the prepared baking sheet. Drizzle with maple syrup (if using) and sprinkle with the spices.

ROAST until tender when pierced with a knife, about 30 minutes.

TRANSFER the apples and figs to a food processor. Add the spinach and amaranth and puree until smooth. Add water in 1-tablespoon increments if a smoother consistency is desired.

IF more texture is desired, do not process the amaranth—simply stir it into the mixture before serving.

TIP: Don't have amaranth on hand? Try swapping out with cooked millet, quinoa, oats, or rice.

TIDBIT: Three large fresh figs contain 5.5 grams of dietary fiber. That's more fiber than in 1 cup of cooked oatmeal!

TIDBIT: Nutmeg can be used to help colic.

SUITABLE FOR FREEZING.

super seed blend

MAKES 1 CUP (SIXTEEN 1-TABLESPOON SERVINGS)

Rich in protein, fiber, and omega-3s, this power-house super seed mix can be added to any puree for baby to pack it with extra nutritional punch. These seeds are major contributors to healthy brain and body development, so there's no better time to introduce them to your child's diet.

    ½ cup flax seeds
    ½ cup quinoa
    ¼ cup hemp hearts
    1 tablespoon chia seeds

COMBINE all the ingredients in a high-speed blender or spice grinder and process into a fine powder. Store the ground seeds in a resealable container in the refrigerator.

STIR in 1 tablespoon of seed blend to ½ cup of baby food.

TIP: Blend with fruit purees, yogurt, and smoothies or add to baking recipes for super nutrition.

TIDBIT: Flax seeds are mostly known for their omega-3 fatty acids, but they're also high in calcium and phosphorus, which promote bone development.

TIDBIT: Hemp is one of only a few plant foods that provide all the essential amino acids, making it a complete source of protein.

sweet potatoes, apples, and chicken

MAKES 1 CUP (TWO ½-CUP SERVINGS)

When authorities started recommending that proteins be introduced to baby at six months, we immediately developed a basic recipe combining the texture of chicken with perennial baby favorites sweet potatoes and apples. This recipe is one of our top protein sellers!

    1 large sweet potato, peeled and diced
    2 cups water
    1 apple, peeled, cored, and diced
    ¼ cup cooked chicken breast or thigh, diced

PLACE the sweet potatoes and water in a saucepan. Bring to a boil, then cover, reduce the heat, and simmer for 10 minutes.

ADD the apples, continuing to simmer for an additional 10 minutes, or until fork-soft. Drain, reserving all the cooking liquid.

TRANSFER the sweet potatoes and apples to a blender, along with 1 cup of the cooking water. Add the chicken and puree until very smooth. Add more water in 1-tablespoon increments if necessary.

TIDBIT: Chicken is packed with protein, which helps babies grow strong.

SUITABLE FOR FREEZING.

minty green pea and barley puree

MAKES 3 CUPS (SIX ½-CUP SERVINGS)

1 tablespoon olive oil
½ small onion, chopped
1 small garlic clove, minced
1½ cups low-sodium vegetable stock
1½ cups shelled garden peas
3 or 4 fresh mint leaves
¼ cup Greek yogurt
½ cup cooked barley

HEAT the olive oil in a medium saucepan over medium-high heat. Add the onion and cook until it softens, about 5 minutes. Add the garlic and cook until fragrant, about 1 minute. Add the stock, peas, and mint. Cover, reduce the heat to medium-low, and simmer for 5 to 6 minutes. Remove from the heat.

ADD the Greek yogurt to the pot. Using an immersion or standard blender, puree until smooth. Stir in the barley and serve.

FOR a more blended texture, pulse the combination in a food processor until a smoother consistency is reached.

TIDBIT: Refreshing and bright, mint is a flavorful addition to baby food that can also help soothe tummy aches.

Replace the Greek yogurt with coconut cream for a dairy alternative.

SUITABLE FOR FREEZING.

vanilla banana berry risotto

MAKES 1½ CUPS (THREE ½-CUP SERVINGS)

Another classic recipe from Baby Gourmet, this has a delightful texture for babies just learning to smack.

> ½ cup blueberries, fresh or frozen
> ½ cup water
> ½ teaspoon vanilla
> 2 bananas, sliced
> ½ cup cooked brown rice

IN a small saucepan, combine the blueberries, water, and vanilla. Over medium-high heat, bring to a boil. Reduce the heat, cover, and simmer for 7 minutes.

TRANSFER the blueberries, water, and vanilla to a high-speed blender, along with the bananas and rice; pulse until a smooth yet slightly chunky texture is reached. Add more water in 1-tablespoon increments if necessary.

TIDBIT: Blueberries are one of the only natural occurrences of true blue in nature. These super berries contain more antioxidants than most fruits and vegetables. The deep blue comes from flavonoids, which are good for baby's eyes, brain, and urinary tract.

SUITABLE FOR FREEZING.

root veggies and beef

MAKES 2 CUPS (FOUR ½-CUP SERVINGS)

> 2 large potatoes, peeled and diced
> 3 large carrots, peeled and diced
> ½ cup cooked ground beef

PLACE the potatoes and carrots in a saucepan with water to cover. Bring to a boil and cook until fork-tender, about 20 minutes.

DRAIN, reserving all the cooking liquid. Transfer the potatoes and carrots to a high-speed blender, along with the beef and 1 cup of the cooking water, and puree until very smooth. Add more water in 1-tablespoon increments if necessary.

TIDBIT: The iron in beef helps build red blood cells and is needed for baby's brain development and energy.

SUITABLE FOR FREEZING.

wild cod, potatoes, and summer squash

MAKES 4 CUPS (EIGHT ½-CUP SERVINGS)

1 wild cod fillet

2 medium summer squash, cut into 1-inch chunks

½ pound small potatoes, scrubbed and cut into 1-inch chunks

1 small white onion, cut into 1-inch chunks

1 teaspoon fresh thyme leaves

1 tablespoon olive oil

½ lemon, sliced

PREHEAT the oven to 400°F.

RINSE the cod fillet and pat dry; set aside. Line a baking sheet with parchment paper.

ARRANGE the squash, potatoes, onions, and thyme on the prepared baking sheet. Drizzle with the olive oil.

ROAST for 18 minutes, then add the fillet to the baking sheet. Top the fish with lemon slices and bake for another 10 minutes, until the potatoes are tender when pierced with a knife and the fish easily flakes with a fork.

DISCARD the lemon. Transfer the fish, potatoes, onions, squash, and thyme to a food processor and puree until smooth. Add water or milk in 1-tablespoon increments if a smoother consistency is desired.

TIDBIT: Cod is a mild fish and an excellent source of protein, which babies go through quickly as they grow and develop.

SUITABLE FOR FREEZING.

chapter 6

adventurous eaters:
8 months+

Around this age, babies will have mastered more of an up-and-down chewing pattern and greater lip and tongue control. They will be able to push food around in their mouth and will move from feeding themselves with their whole fist (the palmar grasp), to a finer pincer grasp with the thumb and forefinger, making it easier to pick up smaller pieces of food.

Providing some soft textures and finger foods will encourage your baby to practice these munching skills. Many of the recipes in this section will help your adventurous eater get a better hang of self-feeding, like the Banana Bites (page 135), Spiced Pumpkin Flax Teething Biscuits (page 140), Fruity Breadsticks (page 138), and Sweet Potato Mac and Cheese (page 134). If baby tries grabbing the feeding spoon from you at this stage, let him! Select recipes that are a bit stickier, so the food has a greater chance of making it to baby's mouth, like the Roasted Sweet Potato Parsnip Coconut Mash (page 103) or Banana Fig Oatmeal (page 119).

At this age, your baby is still breastfeeding but can also have a regular breakfast, lunch, and dinner of solids. Let baby join in your family mealtime. If your baby has not been keen on solids up to this point, try again at a time when your baby has more appetite—maybe in the morning or before (not after) a milk feeding. While you can still offer your little one pureed foods at this stage, be sure to integrate some textures and finger foods as well, as exposure to a wide range of food is important in this formative time.

gingery pear amaranth porridge

MAKES 3 CUPS (SIX ½-CUP SERVINGS)

> ½ cup amaranth seeds
> 1 pear, peeled, seeded, and grated
> ¼ teaspoon fresh ginger, peeled and grated (or a pinch dried ginger)
> 2 cups water
> Coconut milk

COMBINE the amaranth seeds, pear, ginger, and water in a small saucepan. Bring to a boil over medium heat, then lower the heat to a simmer and cook, stirring until creamy, 20 to 25 minutes.

IF the porridge seems too thick, add more water or coconut milk 1 tablespoon at a time.

TOP with coconut milk before serving.

TIDBIT: Amaranth is a gluten-free whole grain that is naturally high in magnesium, iron, and B vitamins.

avocado scrambled eggs

MAKES 1 SERVING

> 1 large egg
> 1 teaspoon water
> 1 teaspoon coconut oil
> ¼ avocado, peeled, pitted, and diced

CRACK the egg into a bowl. Add the water and whisk until the egg looks foamy and light.

HEAT a small nonstick skillet over medium heat. Melt the coconut oil, then turn the heat down to low and slowly pour in the egg. Using a heat-resistant rubber spatula, slowly stir the egg from the outside of the pan to the center. Once the egg begins to set, stir in the diced avocado.

TIDBIT: Eggs provide a perfect balance of amino acids and are the "gold-star" protein. Egg yolks are high in iron and other nutrients, while the whites are high in protein. You can introduce both egg whites and yolks to baby at six months.

berry bircher muesli

MAKES 2 CUPS (FOUR ½-CUP SERVINGS)

I keep this hearty breakfast readily available in my fridge, as it makes a handy snack. I like to store it in mini mason jars for a quick grab-and-go meal. If I'm feeling particularly hungry or know it'll be a while before my next meal, I'll add sliced almonds and shredded coconut.

  1 cup old-fashioned rolled oats
  1 apple, peeled, cored, and grated
  ¾ teaspoon cinnamon
  ¾ cup unsweetened apple juice or orange juice
  ¾ cup plain Greek yogurt
  1 tablespoon flax seeds or hemp seeds
  Fresh berries, for serving

IN a medium bowl, combine the oats, apple, cinnamon, juice, yogurt, and seeds.

COVER and place in the refrigerator for 6 to 8 hours, or overnight. Top with fresh berries before serving.

TIP: To make a more grown-up version, try adding shredded coconut and sliced almonds.

TIDBIT: Greek yogurt has double the protein and half the sugar of most regular yogurts. That said, always read the labels, as some "Greek-style" yogurts have additives that make them less healthy.

To make gluten-free, use gluten-free oats.

To make dairy-free and vegan, substitute the Greek yogurt with coconut milk yogurt or a dairy-free alternative.

Keep stored in the refrigerator for up to 3 days.

peanut butter and banana hot quinoa cereal

MAKES 2 CUPS (FOUR ½-CUP SERVINGS)

This delicious cereal tastes like a peanut butter sandwich and is a great way to integrate peanuts into your baby's diet. There's no evidence that delaying the introduction of peanuts and nuts beyond six months helps to prevent allergies—in fact, it may cause them! Introducing peanuts earlier (anytime after six months) and feeding them to baby a few times per week can help to promote tolerance.

    1 cup unsweetened almond milk
    ⅓ cup quinoa flakes
    1 small ripe banana, mashed
    1 tablespoon peanut butter

IN a small to medium saucepan, bring the milk to a gentle boil, stir in the quinoa flakes, and turn off the heat.

LET sit for 3 minutes, stirring occasionally.

STIR in the mashed bananas and peanut butter.

TIP: Try almond or cashew butter with diced strawberries for a new flavor variety.

TIDBIT: Peanut butter is a nutritional powerhouse, providing protein, beneficial fatty acids, vitamin E, and important minerals.

indian spiced yogurt

MAKES 1½ CUPS (THREE ½-CUP SERVINGS)

1½ cups Greek yogurt
3 tablespoons coconut milk
⅛ teaspoon turmeric
1/16 teaspoon cinnamon
1/16 teaspoon cardamom
1/16 teaspoon nutmeg
Banana slices, for serving (optional)
1 teaspoon maple syrup, for serving (optional)

COMBINE all the ingredients.

TOP with banana slices and maple syrup if desired.

TIP: If the consistency is too thin, stir in a tablespoon of baby cereal.

TIDBIT: Turmeric has been used in India for thousands of years as a spice and medicinal herb. It contains curcumin, which has powerful anti-inflammatory and antioxidant properties and may aid in digestion.

creamy bananas and quinoa

MAKES ONE ½-CUP SERVING

½ banana
3 tablespoons cooked quinoa
1 tablespoon Greek yogurt
Pinch of cinnamon

PLACE the banana in a bowl and mash with a fork.

ADD the remaining ingredients and stir to combine. Serve.

TIP: Don't make a big batch of this one, and what you do make, eat soon after. The bananas brown, and the yogurt does not freeze and thaw well. This one tastes best when consumed the same day.

TIDBIT: Ideal for vegetarian babies, quinoa has a higher protein content than any grain and contains all the essential amino acids.

banana fig oatmeal

MAKES 2 CUPS (FOUR ½-CUP SERVINGS)

I find this meal to be the epitome of comfort food, as it brings back such wonderful memories of the early days in Baby Gourmet's kitchen. This always went up on the menu board as the first recipe for the day. We would make extra for ourselves, and the chop-and-chat ladies would hover around our lunch table and savor a warm bowl of this oatmeal. Add half-and-half as an optional topping for serving.

> 1½ cups milk, water, coconut milk, or almond milk
> 2 large dried figs, chopped
> ½ teaspoon cinnamon
> 1 cup old-fashioned rolled oats
> 1 ripe banana, mashed
> Greek yogurt, banana slices, and maple syrup, for serving (optional)

IN a medium saucepan, bring the milk, figs, and cinnamon to a gentle boil. Stir in the oats.

RETURN to a boil, then reduce the heat to medium. Cook for 5 minutes, stirring occasionally until the liquid is absorbed.

REMOVE from the heat. Stir in the mashed bananas.

TOP with a dollop of yogurt, banana slices, and 1 tablespoon maple syrup if desired.

TIDBIT: Babies' digestive systems are not yet well developed, so soft figs can help them digest food and absorb nutrients better.

Can be made dairy-free and vegan by using coconut, almond, or rice milk.

Can be made gluten-free by using certified gluten-free oats.

SUITABLE FOR FREEZING
(may require additional liquid when reheated).

raspberry coconut chia pudding

MAKES 3 CUPS (SIX ½-CUP SERVINGS)

Healthy fats, protein, and fiber make this creamy treat perfect for babies. And the flavors are so luscious, I can guarantee that you will be sneaking some of this one for yourself!

    1 banana
    1 cup raspberries, fresh or frozen
    One (14-ounce) can coconut milk
    ¼ cup water
    ¼ cup chia seeds

IN a high-speed blender, combine all the ingredients and blend until smooth, 30 to 45 seconds. Transfer the pudding to a resealable container, cover, and refrigerate.

TIP: Chia swells in liquid and thickens over time, creating that thick pudding texture. But if the pudding gets too thick, add more water in 1-tablespoon increments to thin out the consistency.

TIP: Replace the coconut milk with water if desired.

TIP: Substitute the raspberries with strawberries or blueberries and add a pinch of cinnamon or vanilla for a new flavor.

TIDBIT: In Thailand, a baby's first solid food is three spoonfuls of coconut flesh, fed to the baby by a Buddhist priest.

seasonal fruit compote

MAKES 4 CUPS (EIGHT ½-CUP SERVINGS)

We used to prepare this recipe as our weekend sampler at the farmers' market. The sweet, warming smell of mulled cinnamon and fruits never failed to draw a crowd of moms and babies to the booth.

    ½ cup dried figs, finely diced
    ½ cup dried apricots, finely diced
    ¼ cup unsweetened dried cranberries
    2 cups water
    1 cup applesauce
    ½ cup oats
    ½ teaspoon cinnamon

IN a medium saucepan, place the figs, apricots, cranberries, and water. Bring to a gentle boil, stirring occasionally. Reduce the heat, add the applesauce, and cover for 5 minutes.

REMOVE from the heat and stir in the oats and cinnamon. Cover the pot and let stand for 20 minutes.

IF the texture at this point is too thick, mash with a fork to a smooth consistency. Add water in 1-tablespoon increments if a smoother texture is desired.

TIP: Be sure to use organic, unsweetened dried fruit when possible. Nonorganic are typically treated with sulfites.

TIDBIT: Cinnamon supports baby's good digestive health, and its lively scent can help boost brain function.

SUITABLE FOR FREEZING.

cardamom coconut rice pudding

MAKES 4 CUPS (EIGHT ½-CUP SERVINGS)

Rice pudding is beloved as a comfort food the world over, and this Indian-styled version is a fun way to introduce new flavors. My mom asks me to make this for her when she comes to town, which goes to show that this one is not just for babies!

 1 cup brown basmati or long grain rice
 1 cup water
 Two (14-ounce) cans coconut milk
 ½ teaspoon salt
 1-inch piece of fresh ginger, peeled and thinly sliced
 6 cardamom pods, crushed, or ½ teaspoon ground cardamom
 3-inch cinnamon stick
 1 tablespoon agave or maple syrup

RINSE the basmati rice and place in a heavy-bottomed saucepan. Add the water, 1 can of coconut milk, salt, ginger, cardamom, and cinnamon. Bring to a boil, reduce the heat to low, and cover for 45 minutes.

STIR in the second can of coconut milk and the syrup, then simmer without a lid over low heat. Cook until the liquid evaporates and the pudding thickens, about 30 minutes. Remove the ginger slices and cinnamon stick.

ALLOW to cool for a few minutes before serving.

TIP: Top with fresh diced mango, bananas, papaya, or fresh figs.

TIDBIT: Cardamom is related to ginger and can be used in similar ways to counteract digestive problems.

Keep stored in the refrigerator for up to 3 days.

SUITABLE FOR FREEZING.

sweet potatoes, miso, and quinoa

MAKES 3 CUPS (SIX ½-CUP SERVINGS)

1 tablespoon olive oil
½ small onion, chopped
1 teaspoon fresh ginger, peeled and minced
1 garlic clove, minced
1 medium sweet potato, peeled and cubed
2 cups water
2 tablespoons white miso paste
1 cup cooked quinoa

HEAT the olive oil in a medium saucepan over medium-high heat. Add the onion and cook until it softens, about 5 minutes. Add the ginger and garlic and cook until fragrant, about 1 minute. Add the sweet potatoes and water, cover, and reduce the heat to medium-low. Simmer until the sweet potatoes are completely tender, about 20 minutes. Remove from the heat.

STIR in the miso. Using an immersion or standard blender, puree the soup until smooth. Mix in the cooked quinoa. Serve.

TIP: White miso works best in this recipe, as its color is more appealing, but red or black miso will work fine if you have them on hand.

TIP: Stir in a tablespoon of Greek yogurt and a pinch of finely chopped cilantro for a twist.

TIDBIT: Miso is a traditional Japanese food that's prepared by fermenting rice, soy, or barley. It is high in protein and rich in vitamins and minerals. Miso is a wonderful probiotic food that aids digestion and intestinal issues, and ginger has properties known to settle an upset tummy.

SUITABLE FOR FREEZING.

savory parmesan millet porridge

MAKES 2 CUPS (FOUR ½-CUP SERVINGS)

- ⅓ cup raw millet
- 2 teaspoons butter, divided
- 1¼ cups sodium-reduced chicken broth
- 1 tablespoon Parmesan cheese, grated
- 1 teaspoon fresh parsley, finely chopped

IN a small food processor or coffee grinder, pulse the millet until coarsely ground.

MELT 1 teaspoon butter in a small saucepan over medium heat. Once bubbling, add the ground millet and stir for 2 to 3 minutes to lightly toast.

SLOWLY stir in the chicken broth, bringing to a simmer and stirring occasionally, then stir until fully combined and creamy.

REDUCE the heat to low and cover, simmering for 8 to 10 minutes. Do not stir while it cooks. The consistency should be creamy and thick but still pourable. If it appears too runny, put the lid back on for 3 more minutes. If it is too thick, add a little stock to thin it out.

REMOVE from the heat, stir in the Parmesan, the remaining 1 teaspoon butter, and parsley. Allow to rest for 3 to 4 minutes to thicken. Serve.

TIDBIT: Millet is a gluten-free ancient grain that is especially high in the B vitamins folate, B_6, thiamine, and riboflavin, all important for baby's growth.

veggie lentil dal

MAKES 4 CUPS (EIGHT ½-CUP SERVINGS)

- 1 tablespoon olive oil
- 1 small onion, diced
- 1 teaspoon cinnamon
- ½ teaspoon cumin
- ¼ teaspoon coriander
- 1 cup red lentils, rinsed
- 4 cups water
- 1 medium butternut squash, peeled, seeded, and diced

IN a large saucepan, heat the oil over medium-high heat. Sauté the onion until soft, about 3 minutes. Toss in the spices and sauté for another minute, until fragrant.

ADD the lentils and water and bring to a boil. Add the butternut squash and bring back to a boil. Cover, reduce the heat, and simmer for 15 minutes, until the squash is fork-tender.

REMOVE from the heat and drain, reserving all the cooking liquid. Add the mixture to a food processor. Pulse, adding the cooking water as needed, until a desired consistency is reached.

TIDBIT: Cumin is another spice that aids digestion. It's thought that the seeds also have anticarcinogenic properties.

SUITABLE FOR FREEZING.

mediterranean chicken

MAKES 4 CUPS (EIGHT ½-CUP SERVINGS)

1 tablespoon olive oil

1 green onion, white part only, sliced

1 carrot, peeled and sliced

½ red pepper, diced

½ zucchini, quartered and sliced

4 mushrooms, peeled and sliced

½ pound boneless, skinless chicken breast, chopped

½ teaspoon ground rosemary

One (28-ounce) can plum tomatoes

½ cup green beans, chopped

1 cup cooked brown rice or quinoa

IN a medium saucepan, heat the oil over medium-high heat. Sauté the green onion, carrot, pepper, zucchini, mushrooms, chicken, and rosemary until soft, 3 to 5 minutes.

ADD the tomatoes and bring to a gentle boil. Add the green beans and cooked rice and cover, simmering for 20 minutes.

REMOVE from the heat and transfer the mixture to a food processor. Pulse until the desired consistency is reached. If the texture is too thick, add water in 1-tablespoon increments until the preferred texture is reached.

TIDBIT: Chicken is packed with protein and is a good source of vitamin B_6, which helps babies extract energy from food.

To make this recipe vegetarian and vegan, remove the chicken or substitute with cooked lentils.

SUITABLE FOR FREEZING.

wild salmon with potatoes, leeks, and spinach

MAKES 3 CUPS (SIX ½-CUP SERVINGS)

This was one of our first recipes from the farmers' market. Parents loved that it gave them an easy way to introduce omega-3-rich salmon and power-packed spinach into their babies' diets.

- 1 tablespoon olive oil
- 1 leek, white part only, sliced
- 1 large potato, peeled and grated
- 1 cup milk
- ½ pound fresh wild salmon, skin removed
- 2 cups spinach, chopped

IN a medium saucepan, heat the oil over medium-high heat. Sauté the leeks until soft, about 3 minutes. Add the grated potatoes and sauté for an additional 5 minutes.

ADD the milk and bring to a gentle boil. Add the salmon and spinach, cover, and reduce the heat. Steam for 5 to 8 minutes, until the fish is cooked through.

REMOVE from the heat and transfer the mixture to a food processor. Pulse until the desired consistency is reached. If the texture is too thick, add milk in 1-tablespoon increments until the optimal texture is reached.

TIDBIT: The omega-3s in fish can help babies with eczema or other skin ailments.

Can be made dairy-free by substituting water or a dairy alternative for the milk.

SUITABLE FOR FREEZING.

lemon parmesan broccoli and chicken

MAKES 4 CUPS (EIGHT ½-CUP SERVINGS)

I like to make a little extra of this one and have it for dinner myself—obviously without the puree-ing!

- 1 pound broccoli, separated into florets
- 1 garlic clove, sliced
- 2 tablespoons olive oil, divided
- Juice of 1 lemon, divided
- One 5-ounce boneless, skinless chicken breast
- ¼ cup Parmesan cheese, grated

PREHEAT the oven to 425°F. Line a baking sheet with parchment paper.

PLACE the broccoli and garlic on the prepared baking sheet. Toss with 1 tablespoon oil and half of the lemon juice until evenly distributed.

PLACE the chicken breast next to the broccoli and drizzle with remaining oil and lemon juice.

ROAST in the oven for 20 to 25 minutes.

PLACE the roasted broccoli, chicken, juices, and Parmesan cheese in a food processor. Pulse, adding water in 1-tablespoon increments, until a desired consistency is reached.

TIP: Try using milk instead of water for a creamier texture.

TIDBIT: Broccoli can help boost a baby's immune system, making baby less prone to coughs and colds.

SUITABLE FOR FREEZING.

moroccan lamb with couscous

MAKES 4 CUPS (EIGHT ½-CUP SERVINGS)

1 small butternut squash, peeled, seeded, and diced
1 cup couscous
1 tablespoon olive oil
1 small onion, diced
½ red pepper, diced
½ zucchini, quartered and sliced
½ pound ground lamb
½ teaspoon cinnamon
¼ teaspoon cumin
1 tablespoon cilantro, chopped (or 1 teaspoon dried)

IN a large pot, bring water to a boil. Add the butternut squash and continue to boil until fork-tender, 10 to 15 minutes. Drain, reserving the cooking liquid to prepare the couscous.

IN a large bowl, combine the couscous and 1½ cups of the cooking water. Cover and let stand for 5 minutes, then fluff with a fork.

IN a medium saucepan, heat the oil over medium-high heat. Sauté the onion, pepper, and zucchini until soft, 3 to 5 minutes.

ADD the lamb and spices and cook for about 8 minutes, until cooked through.

PLACE the cooked lamb and butternut squash in a food processor, pureeing until smooth. Add the cooking liquid in 1-tablespoon increments to create a smooth texture.

IN a large bowl, mix the lamb and squash puree with the couscous. Serve.

Can be made gluten-free by substituting the couscous with quinoa or another gluten-free ancient grain.

SUITABLE FOR FREEZING.

one-pot turkey, veggies, and brown rice

MAKES 4 CUPS (EIGHT ½-CUP SERVINGS)

This is a big recipe for a reason: I like to eat it myself! Not only is it a great baby food, it's a yummy, healthy lunch for me. I freeze the leftovers for single-serve portions.

3 cups low-sodium chicken broth
1 cup brown basmati rice
½ pound ground turkey
½ medium onion, diced
2 medium carrots, peeled and chopped
1 head broccoli, chopped
¼ cup frozen peas
3 garlic cloves, diced
1 teaspoon sea salt
1 teaspoon pepper
2 tablespoons butter

ADD all the ingredients in a large saucepan. Turn the heat on high and bring to a boil. Stir once to get everything evenly dispersed, then cover and cook for about 50 minutes.

IF the texture is too chunky for baby, pulse or puree in a food processor with some liquid until the desired consistency is reached.

COOL before serving.

TIP: Use 1 cup of shredded leftover turkey or chicken if you have it on hand.

TIDBIT: Turkey makes a great first meat for baby. It's high in protein and iron and is easily digested.

Can be made dairy-free by replacing the butter with coconut or olive oil.

SUITABLE FOR FREEZING.

beef bolognese with pasta stars

MAKES 4 CUPS (EIGHT ½-CUP SERVINGS)

1 tablespoon olive oil
1 small onion, finely chopped
2 carrots, peeled and sliced
1 celery stalk, sliced
4 mushrooms, peeled and sliced
½ pound ground beef
One (28-ounce) can crushed tomatoes
1 teaspoon dried basil
1 cup cooked pasta stars

IN a medium saucepan, heat the oil over medium-high heat. Sauté the onion, carrots, celery, and mushrooms for 3 to 5 minutes. Add the ground beef and cook another 6 to 8 minutes, until cooked through.

ADD the tomatoes and basil and bring to a gentle boil. Reduce the heat and simmer for 15 minutes, stirring occasionally.

REMOVE from the heat and transfer the beef mixture to a food processor, pureeing until smooth. If the texture is too thick, add water in 1-tablespoon increments until the optimal texture is reached.

STIR in the cooked pasta. Serve.

TIDBIT: Tomatoes are rich in vitamin C, which can help your baby absorb more iron from other foods.

SUITABLE FOR FREEZING.

coconut chicken curry

MAKES 6 CUPS (TWELVE ½-CUP SERVINGS)

Remember, not all baby food needs to be only for baby. This is one for the whole family!

- 1 tablespoon olive oil
- 1 medium onion, chopped
- 1 garlic clove, minced
- 1 tablespoon fresh ginger, peeled and minced
- 2 large carrots, peeled and sliced
- 2 tablespoons mild curry paste
- 1½ pounds boneless, skinless chicken breast, diced into ½-inch pieces
- 1 cup low-sodium chicken broth
- One (14-ounce) can coconut milk
- 1 large Granny Smith apple, peeled, cored, and cut into small chunks
- 1 cup frozen edamame or peas
- 3 cups cooked brown rice

IN a large saucepan, heat the oil over medium-high heat. Sauté the onion, garlic, ginger, and carrots for 2 minutes. Add the curry paste and cook, stirring until fragrant, about 2 minutes. Add the chicken, stir to coat it in the spices, and brown for 5 minutes.

ADD the broth and coconut milk; cook on medium-low for 10 minutes to thicken. Add the apples and peas; cook for an additional 5 minutes, or until cooked through.

SERVE the chicken curry over brown rice.

TIDBIT: Edamame is a complete protein containing all nine essential amino acids that offers a protein profile equal to both meat and eggs.

To make this recipe vegetarian and vegan, omit the chicken or substitute with cubed tofu.

SUITABLE FOR FREEZING.

sweet potato mac and cheese

MAKES 4 CUPS (EIGHT ½-CUP SERVINGS)

A lovely homemade introduction to mac and cheese that baby will not be able to resist. When my kids were introduced to boxed mac and cheese at a friend's house, they asked if I could buy some. Not willing to buy the boxes, I came up with this recipe (which looks exactly like the boxed stuff) and convinced them it wasn't homemade. They bought the story, but only for a few years, until they were around seven. Now they know the difference but still love my version at ages eight and nine.

> ½ pound brown rice elbow pasta
> 4 cups sweet potatoes, peeled and chopped
> 2 cups milk
> 1 tablespoon butter
> 1 cup cheddar cheese, grated

BRING a large pot of salted water to a boil. Add the pasta and cook until al dente, then drain and set aside.

IN a large saucepan over medium-low heat, combine the sweet potatoes, milk, and butter. Cover and simmer for 20 minutes, until the sweet potatoes are tender. Remove from the heat and let cool for 5 minutes.

TRANSFER the sweet potato mixture to a food processor. Add the cheese and puree until smooth.

COMBINE the sweet potato mixture with the cooked pasta. Put the mac and cheese back into the food processor and pulse until a desired chunky texture is reached. Add milk in 1-tablespoon increments if a thinner consistency is desired.

TIDBIT: Sweet potatoes are a baby superfood, rich in beta-carotene, which is important for good vision, healthy skin, and protection from infections.

SUITABLE FOR FREEZING.

banana bites

MAKES 8 BANANA BITES

My kids loved these bite-size banana pancakes, especially when they dipped them in syrup. Today my kids are old enough to make them for themselves.

½ cup whole wheat flour
2 tablespoons flax meal
½ teaspoon baking powder
¼ teaspoon baking soda
Pinch of sea salt
1 egg
½ cup milk
3 teaspoons butter or coconut oil, melted
¼ teaspoon vanilla
Cooking spray
1 large banana, sliced diagonally in ½-inch pieces

IN a medium bowl, combine the flour, flax meal, baking powder, baking soda, and salt.

IN a small bowl, whisk together the egg, milk, melted butter, and vanilla. Add to the dry ingredients and stir until moistened.

HEAT a nonstick pan or prep a griddle with cooking spray over medium heat.

DIP each banana slice into the pancake batter and coat both sides. Place the coated banana slices onto the hot pan, browning each side for about 2 minutes. Serve.

TIP: Try serving with a side of warmed maple syrup that baby can dip into.

TIDBIT: Fully ripe bananas are better for eating, as they contain more antioxidants than under-ripe fruit. (And they're sweeter!)

Can be made gluten-free by substituting the flour with an all-purpose gluten-free blend.

mini pumpkin patties

MAKES 16 PATTIES

One (15-ounce) can pumpkin puree
½ cup spelt flour, whole wheat flour, or a
gluten-free flour blend
1 egg, beaten
1 tablespoon maple syrup
1 teaspoon baking powder
¼ teaspoon salt
2 tablespoons butter
2 tablespoons coconut oil
½ teaspoon cinnamon
2 tablespoons maple flakes or cane sugar

IN a large bowl, combine the pumpkin, flour, egg, maple syrup, baking powder, and salt.

HEAT 1 tablespoon of the butter and 1 tablespoon of the oil in a large skillet over medium heat. Drop 8 patties (1 tablespoon each) into the hot pan and lightly flatten them with a spatula. Cook until golden, about 4 minutes per side.

REPEAT for the second batch.

MIX the cinnamon and maple flakes and sprinkle over the warm patties before serving.

TIP: Don't have pumpkin puree? Try using mashed sweet potatoes.

TIDBIT: The beta-carotene form of vitamin A in pumpkin is good for baby's eyesight development.

Can be made gluten-free by substituting flour with a gluten-free blend.

Can be made dairy-free by using all coconut oil instead of half butter.

Store in the refrigerator for up to 3 days.

SUITABLE FOR FREEZING.

cheesy herb breadsticks

MAKES THIRTY 7-INCH BREADSTICKS

2 cups whole wheat flour
1 teaspoon active dry yeast
1 teaspoon sugar
⅔ cup warm water
2½ teaspoons salt
3 teaspoons dried basil
1½ cups grated cheese

MEASURE the flour into a mixing bowl, add the remaining ingredients, and mix until the dough is soft and comes away from the sides of the bowl.

TURN the dough onto a floured work surface and knead for about 2 minutes. Add more flour if needed to prevent sticking. Return the dough to the bowl, cover with a damp kitchen towel or plastic wrap, and let rise at room temperature until doubled in size, approximately one hour.

PREHEAT the oven to 375°F. Line a baking sheet with parchment paper.

TURN the dough onto a floured work surface and knead for a few more minutes, adding more flour if it's too sticky. Divide the dough into 30 small balls and roll each into a long, thin stick using the palm of your hand. Place the sticks on the prepared baking sheet and leave in a warm place for 20 minutes.

BAKE in the oven for 15 to 20 minutes. Cool and serve.

STORE for 1 week in an airtight container or in the freezer for up to 3 months.

TIP: Babies especially love these right out of the freezer—the cold chewiness soothes teething gums.

TIDBIT: Cheese is wonderful for babies, providing calcium, fat, and protein.

SUITABLE FOR FREEZING.

fruity breadsticks

MAKES THIRTY 7-INCH BREADSTICKS

These little breadsticks sold big at the farmers' market. We used to make these by hand, and I still remember the hours of hand-rolling. Like any finger food, breadsticks could be a choking hazard, so be sure to keep an eye on baby.

    2 cups whole wheat flour
    1 teaspoon active dry yeast
    1 teaspoon sugar
    ⅔ cup warm water
    2½ teaspoons salt
    1 cup raisins, chopped

MEASURE the flour into a mixing bowl, add the remaining ingredients, and mix until the dough is soft and comes away from the sides of the bowl.

TURN the dough onto a floured work surface and knead for about 2 minutes. Add more flour if needed to prevent sticking. Return the dough to the bowl, cover with a damp kitchen towel or plastic wrap, and let rise at room temperature until doubled in size, approximately an hour.

PREHEAT the oven to 375°F. Line a baking sheet with parchment paper.

TURN the dough onto a floured work surface and knead for a few more minutes, adding more flour if it's too sticky. Divide the dough into 30 small balls, and roll each piece into a long, thin stick using the palm of your hand. Place the sticks on the prepared baking sheet and leave in a warm place for 20 minutes.

BAKE in the oven for 15 to 20 minutes. Cool and serve.

TIDBIT: Babies love these right out of the freezer. Frozen biscuits and breadsticks cool sore, teething gums and dissolve more slowly.

Store for 1 week in an airtight container or in the freezer for up to 3 months.

spiced pumpkin flax teething biscuits

MAKES 16 BISCUITS

1 cup baby oatmeal cereal

1 cup light spelt or whole wheat flour

2 tablespoons flax meal

2 tablespoons coconut oil, melted

⅓ cup pumpkin puree

2 teaspoons cinnamon

6 to 8 tablespoons water

PREHEAT the oven to 425°F. Line a baking sheet with parchment paper.

MIX all the ingredients in a medium bowl. Mix well until a dough forms. Roll out on a floured surface until ¼ to ½ inch thick. Cut into shapes with a cookie cutter or cut into squares. Place on the prepared baking sheet and bake for 15 to 18 minutes.

LET cool completely.

TIP: Don't have pumpkin puree? Substitute pumpkin with 1 mashed banana or ⅓ cup applesauce or sweet potato puree.

TIDBIT: Flax seeds are one of the best plant sources of omega-3 fatty acids.

Store 1 week in an airtight container or freeze for up to 3 months.

Can be made gluten-free by substituting a gluten-free flour blend.

chapter 7

independent toddlers:
12 months+

At this point, your toddler will be on the same meal pattern as the rest of the family: three meals a day, with a few snacks between. This section contains meal recipes that older children and the adults of the house will enjoy, too, like Blueberry Cottage Cheese Pancakes (page 146) and Sweet Potato Curry (page 152). You'll also find recipes for tasty and nutritious snack ideas, many of which can be taken on the go, including Chocolate Coconut Granola Bars (page 170) and Banana Zucchini Flax Muffins (page 177).

Your independent toddler will want to eat what Mom and Dad are eating—which is often a strong motivator to clean up your own diet! Try to sit at the table and eat as many meals as possible with your little ones. Family mealtimes have huge benefits, especially as your child grows older. This shared mealtime is not just about the food—it's an opportunity for the family to reconnect at the end of a busy day.

On that note, do your best to ensure that mealtimes are pleasant. Your toddler's growth has slowed, so her appetite may as well. She may refuse foods she previously enjoyed. This is totally normal. Remember, it's your job to offer the food, and it's your child's job to determine how much (if any) they will eat. By avoiding rewards, bribes, and pressure, you can help your child grow up with a healthy relationship with food and keep family meals fun.

pumpkin waffles

MAKES 18 WAFFLES

Of all the foods we sold at the farmers' market, these were our number-one seller. Moms came in droves to pick up these freezer-friendly gems. This recipe is doubled, so you can batch freeze the extras and pop them in the toaster for a quick breakfast or on-the-go snack.

  3½ cups milk
  2 cups pumpkin puree
  ¼ cup canola oil
  ½ cup maple syrup
  4 large eggs, lightly beaten
  3 cups unbleached all-purpose flour
  1½ cups whole wheat flour
  2 tablespoons baking powder
  1 teaspoon baking soda
  2 teaspoons ground cinnamon
  ¼ teaspoon salt

PLACE the milk, pumpkin, oil, maple syrup, and eggs in a medium bowl and whisk until smooth.

IN a large bowl, combine the flours, baking powder, baking soda, cinnamon, and salt.

ADD the liquid ingredients into the dry ingredients and whisk until smooth. Preheat the waffle iron. Let the batter rest 5 minutes before using.

POUR the batter into the waffle maker ¼ cup at a time. Bake as timed.

TIP: Freeze by placing wax paper squares in between each waffle; stack them and place in freezer bag.

TIP: Serve warm waffles topped with butter, sliced bananas, walnuts, and a drizzle of maple syrup.

TIDBIT: Maple syrup contains trace minerals and can replace processed sugar when cooking and baking for babies and children.

Can be made gluten-free by substituting both flours with a gluten-free blend.

Can be made dairy-free by substituting the milk with dairy alternatives such as coconut, hemp, or almond milk.

SUITABLE FOR FREEZING.

blueberry cottage cheese pancakes with banana cream

MAKES 24 SMALL PANCAKES

High-protein pancakes are a great way to start the day. They are just as delicious as normal pancakes, but the extra protein will keep you fuller longer. And they're not just for toddlers—I have been known to sneak a few of them myself!

3 eggs
1 cup cottage cheese
1 teaspoon vanilla extract
1 tablespoon honey or maple syrup
½ cup whole wheat flour
1 teaspoon baking powder
Pinch of cinnamon
¼ teaspoon salt
1 cup blueberries, fresh or frozen
Cooking spray

Banana Cream Topping
2 ripe bananas, mashed (you can get your kids to do this part—they love it)
½ cup plain Greek yogurt
Pinch of cinnamon
Maple syrup (optional)

IN a small bowl, combine the eggs, cottage cheese, vanilla, and honey.

IN a medium bowl, combine all the dry ingredients. Stir the wet ingredients into the dry ingredients until moistened. Fold in the blueberries.

PREHEAT the oven to 200°F. Heat a nonstick pan or prep a griddle with cooking spray over medium heat. Use ¼ cup batter for each pancake. Cook until lightly browned on each side, about 2 minutes per side. Keep warm in the oven until all the batter has been used up.

MIX all the ingredients for the banana cream topping.

TOP the pancakes with a dollop of banana cream or use it for dipping.

TIP: Pop frozen pancakes in the toaster for quick morning meals or snacks.

TIDBIT: Cottage cheese is high in protein, which helps build cells, muscles, and organs during this rapid growth stage.

Can be made gluten-free by substituting the flour with an all-purpose gluten-free blend.

SUITABLE FOR FREEZING.

mango carrot smoothie

MAKES 3 SERVINGS

 1 cup mango, frozen diced
 1 banana
 1½ cups fresh carrot juice
 ½ cup vanilla Greek yogurt
 ½ cup ice cubes

PLACE all the ingredients in a high-speed blender and blend until smooth. Serve.

TIP: Reduce the amount of carrot juice for a thicker, spoon-fed meal or add baby cereal for texture. Adding cereal to the smoothie helps boost the iron and vitamin content.

TIDBIT: Carrots are full of vitamin A, which is essential for healthy eyes and skin and helps fight infection.

banana kale smoothie

MAKES 2 CUPS (TWO 1-CUP SERVINGS)

Any time you can get a cup of kale into your little one, it's a bonus. Kale has a strong flavor and a tougher texture than other leafy greens. I find blending it up with creamy bananas and sweet apples makes kale much more palatable. This doesn't mask the flavor as much as soften it, so little ones can start to develop a taste for it gradually.

 2 small bananas
 1 apple, cored and chopped
 1 cup kale, chopped
 1 cup milk, almond milk, or coconut milk
 2 or 3 ice cubes

IN a high-speed blender, combine all the ingredients and blend until smooth.

SERVE immediately or refrigerate for up to 48 hours.

TIP: Toss in a couple tablespoons of added goodness with chia, flax, or hemp seeds.

TIDBIT: Kale is high in vitamin C, which helps babies build healthy bones.

Can be made dairy-free by using a dairy alternative.

spiced apple oatmeal smoothie

MAKES 1 CUP (TWO ½-CUP SERVINGS)

> 1 apple, peeled, cored, and diced
> ¼ cup oats
> ¼ cup kefir or whole milk yogurt
> ¼ cup milk
> Pinch of cinnamon
> 2 ice cubes

PUREE all the ingredients in a high-speed blender until smooth.

SERVE immediately or refrigerate for up to 48 hours.

TIP: Try using fortified baby oatmeal cereal for added iron.

TIDBIT: Kefir offers needed saturated fat and easily digested carbohydrates, as well as healthy active cultures.

Can be made gluten-free by using gluten-free oats.
Can be made dairy-free by using a dairy alternative.

fresh minty pea hummus

MAKES 2 CUPS (EIGHT ¼-CUP SERVINGS)

> 1¼ cups shelled green peas, fresh or frozen, thawed
> 1 cup garbanzo beans, drained and rinsed
> ¼ cup plain Greek yogurt
> 2 tablespoons green onion, chopped
> 3 tablespoons fresh mint, chopped
> 2 tablespoons fresh lemon juice
> ½ teaspoon salt
> Sliced pitas or fresh veggies, for serving

PLACE all the ingredients in a food processor and blend until smooth.

FOR self-feeders, spread bite-size pita pieces with the prepared hummus or allow them to dip the pieces themselves.

TIDBIT: Adding peas to baby's diet can boost fiber intake, lower cholesterol, and keep the heart healthy.

mini spinach ricotta frittatas

MAKES 20 MINI FRITTATAS

Kids love anything bite-size, and these delicious little nibbles are yummy whether served warm or cold, for an on-the-go snack.

2 tablespoons olive oil
1 small onion, finely chopped
1 garlic clove, minced
2 large eggs
1 cup ricotta cheese
½ cup Parmesan cheese, grated
One (10-ounce) package frozen spinach, chopped, thawed, and drained well
¼ teaspoon salt

PREHEAT the oven to 350°F. Lightly grease a mini muffin tin.

IN a small skillet, heat the oil over medium heat and sauté the onion and garlic until tender, 3 to 4 minutes. Set aside to cool.

WHISK the eggs in a bowl and stir in the ricotta and Parmesan cheese. Then stir in the spinach, salt, and onion mixture.

POUR the mixture into the prepared mini muffin cups.

BAKE for 20 to 25 minutes, until the filling is set and lightly browned.

SERVE warm or cold.

TIP: The unbaked frittata mixture can be made 6 hours ahead—just cover and chill.

TIP: For the frittatas to hold together, it's very important to drain the spinach of any excess water. Use paper towels to make sure it's nice and dry.

TIDBIT: Eggs have choline, which plays an important role in brain development.

sweet potato curry

MAKES 4 CUPS (EIGHT ½-CUP SERVINGS)

If you like the combination of peanuts and creamy coconut, then why not introduce it to your little adventurous eater? The flavors are mild yet distinct. This is a big recipe, because you'll want to serve it to the whole family.

1 tablespoon olive oil

1 medium onion, diced

3 garlic cloves, minced

1 teaspoon fresh ginger, peeled and grated

2 teaspoons mild curry paste

2 small sweet potatoes, peeled and diced into ¼-inch cubes

One (19-ounce) can chickpeas, drained and rinsed

One (14-ounce) can coconut milk

1 cup orange juice

½ cup peanut butter or other nut butter

1 teaspoon sea salt

1 cup frozen edamame or green peas

4 cups baby spinach, chopped

¼ cup cilantro, chopped

Squeeze of fresh lime juice

Cooked brown rice, for serving

IN a medium saucepan, heat the oil over medium-high heat. Sauté the onion and garlic until lightly browned, about 5 minutes.

ADD the ginger and curry paste. Cook another few minutes, until the spices are heated through and fragrant.

ADD the sweet potatoes, chickpeas, coconut milk, orange juice, peanut butter, and salt. Bring to a gentle boil, lower the heat, and continue simmering until the sweet potatoes are tender, about 30 minutes.

STIR in the edamame, spinach, cilantro, and lime juice.

SERVE over rice.

TIDBIT: Peanut butter is high in protein, which is important for strengthening your baby's growing muscles.

TIDBIT: Garlic has natural antiviral and antibacterial properties that help prevent the common cold and flu as well as gastric infections.

SUITABLE FOR FREEZING.

creamy butternut squash mac and cheese

MAKES 6 CUPS (TWELVE ½-CUP SERVINGS)

3 cups butternut squash, peeled, seeded, and chopped

1 cup low-sodium vegetable broth

1¾ cups milk

2 garlic cloves

1 pound whole wheat pasta shells or cork-screws

2 tablespoons plain Greek yogurt

1¼ cups cheddar cheese, grated

1 cup pecorino Romano cheese, grated

¼ cup Parmesan cheese, grated and divided

1 teaspoon salt

½ teaspoon pepper

1 teaspoon olive oil

½ cup panko breadcrumbs

2 tablespoons fresh parsley, chopped

PREHEAT the oven to 375°F. Lightly grease a 9 x 13-inch baking dish.

COMBINE the squash, broth, milk, and garlic in a medium saucepan. Bring to a gentle boil on medium-high heat. Reduce the heat and simmer until the squash is tender, approximately 25 minutes. Remove from the heat.

WHILE the squash is cooking, make the pasta according to the package directions; drain and set aside.

PLACE the hot squash mixture in a food processor or blender. Add the Greek yogurt and puree until smooth. Add the cheddar, pecorino, and 2 tablespoons Parmesan and puree until the cheese is melted and combined. Season with the salt and pepper.

ADD the squash mixture to the cooked pasta and stir until combined. Spread the mixture evenly into the prepared 9 x 13-inch baking dish.

HEAT the oil in a medium skillet. Add the panko and cook until golden brown, approximately 2 minutes. Remove from the heat, stir in the remaining 2 tablespoons Parmesan cheese, and sprinkle evenly on top of the hot pasta mixture.

BAKE for 25 minutes, or until bubbly. Remove from the heat and allow to cool slightly; top with fresh parsley.

TIDBIT: The vitamin C and beta-carotene in butternut squash help reduce the effects of asthma.

Can be made gluten-free by substituting the wheat pasta with brown rice pasta or another gluten-free alternative.

SUITABLE FOR FREEZING.

cheesy broccoli and chicken pasta shells

MAKES 6 CUPS (TWELVE ½-CUP SERVINGS)

½ pound whole wheat pasta shells
3 cups broccoli florets
4 large carrots, peeled and finely diced
¾ cup evaporated skim milk
1 cup cheddar cheese, grated
1 cup cooked chicken, cubed
¼ cup breadcrumbs

PREHEAT the oven to 400°F.

BRING a large pot of water to a boil. Add the pasta and cook for 3 minutes, then add the broccoli for the remaining 5 minutes. Drain and set aside.

IN a medium saucepan over medium-low heat, combine the carrots, milk, and ½ cup water. Cover and simmer for 15 minutes, until the carrots soften. Remove from the heat and let cool for 5 minutes, then transfer to a food processor. Add the cheese and puree until smooth. Set aside.

IN an 8 x 10-inch baking dish, combine the broccoli, pasta, chicken, and cheese sauce. Spread the mixture in an even layer and top with the breadcrumbs. Bake for 20 minutes, until the top is browned and bubbly.

ALLOW to cool slightly, then serve.

TIP: Freeze leftovers in a muffin tin, then pop out the portions and store them in a resealable bag to use as quick, ready-to-heat meals.

TIDBIT: The high vitamin C content in broccoli helps baby's body to absorb iron, which is essential for growth.

SUITABLE FOR FREEZING.

creamy turkey noodles

MAKES 6 CUPS (TWELVE ½-CUP SERVINGS)

1 tablespoon butter
1 onion, finely chopped
2 garlic cloves, minced
¾ pound ground turkey
⅓ cup all-purpose flour
1 cup reduced-sodium chicken stock
One (12-ounce) can evaporated milk
1 cup frozen edamame or peas
1 cup aged cheddar cheese, shredded
¼ cup fresh parsley, chopped
4 teaspoons Dijon mustard
¼ teaspoon salt and pepper
2 cups whole wheat elbow macaroni

IN a large saucepan, melt the butter over medium heat and cook the onion until translucent, about 2 minutes. Add the garlic; cook for 1 minute.

ADD the turkey. Brown, breaking it up with the back of a spoon, for about 4 minutes. Stir in the flour, then cook, stirring, another 2 minutes. Stir in the broth and evaporated milk; bring to a boil. Reduce the heat to medium, then stir in the edamame, cheese, parsley, mustard, salt, and pepper.

MEANWHILE, bring a large pot of water to a boil. Add the pasta and cook according to the package directions. Drain, reserving ⅓ cup of the cooking liquid. Add the pasta to the sauce, tossing to coat and adding enough of the reserved cooking liquid for the desired consistency.

TIDBIT: Turkey is packed with nutrients important for growth, building and repairing body tissues, and immunity.

SUITABLE FOR FREEZING.

crispy cheese, quinoa, and broccoli bites

MAKES 8 PATTIES

2 tablespoons olive oil
½ medium onion, chopped
2 garlic cloves, minced
2 cups fresh broccoli
¾ cup cooked quinoa
½ cup cheddar cheese, grated
½ cup Parmesan cheese, grated
2 large eggs, beaten
Salt and pepper to taste

PREHEAT the oven to 400°F. Line a baking sheet with parchment paper.

IN a small skillet, heat the oil over medium-high heat. Sauté the onion and garlic until lightly browned, about 5 minutes. Set aside.

IN a food processor, combine the garlic, onion, broccoli, quinoa, cheeses, eggs, salt, and pepper. Pulse until the broccoli is finely chopped.

FORM into patties and place on the prepared baking sheet. Bake for 15 minutes. Flip the patties and bake for an additional 15 minutes, until browned and crispy.

TIP: Try serving this healthy on-the-go snack with a side of avocado cream dipping sauce: ½ mashed avocado, 2 tablespoons Greek yogurt, and a squeeze of lime juice.

TIDBIT: Quinoa is high in the flavonoid quercetin, which is an antioxidant.

SUITABLE FOR FREEZING.

peas, pancetta, and parmesan orzo

MAKES 6 CUPS (TWELVE ½-CUP SERVINGS)

3 tablespoons butter
⅓ cup shallots (about 3), finely diced
1½ cups orzo
3 cups chicken broth
3 ounces pancetta (Italian bacon), chopped (about ½ cup)
1 cup shelled fresh peas or frozen petite peas, thawed
½ cup Parmesan cheese, grated, plus more for sprinkling
4 tablespoons fresh dill, chopped
Salt and pepper to taste

MELT the butter in a skillet over medium-high heat. Sauté the shallots for 2 minutes, then add the orzo and sauté for another 2 minutes, until slightly browned. Add the broth and bring to a boil. Reduce the heat, cover, and simmer until the orzo is tender and the liquid is absorbed, about 20 minutes.

MEANWHILE, in another skillet, sauté the pancetta over medium-high heat until brown, about 4 minutes. Set aside.

ADD the peas and Parmesan to the orzo and combine.

STIR in the cooked pancetta and fresh dill and season with salt and pepper. Sprinkle with a little extra Parmesan and serve.

TIP: Don't have pancetta? Try swapping out with cooked nitrate-free bacon.

TIDBIT: Peas are bursting with vitamin K, a nutrient that works with calcium to help build healthy bones.

Can be made gluten-free by using gluten-free pasta.

SUITABLE FOR FREEZING.

fennel and green pea risotto with goat cheese

MAKES 4 CUPS (EIGHT ½-CUP SERVINGS)

This creamy comfort food will get your family through the winter. Use fresh veggies come the spring.

> 4 cups vegetable broth
> 1 tablespoon olive oil
> 1 fennel bulb, thinly sliced and diced
> 2 garlic cloves, minced
> 1 cup Arborio rice
> 4 ounces soft goat cheese
> 1 cup peas, fresh or frozen, thawed
> 1 tomato, seeded and diced
> 2 tablespoons fresh basil, chopped
> Salt and pepper to taste

IN a large saucepan, bring the broth to a boil. Reduce the heat to a simmer and cover.

HEAT the oil in a deep, heavy saucepan over medium heat. Add the fennel, garlic, and rice. Cook for 5 minutes, until the rice is golden brown. Begin adding the simmering broth to the rice, ½ cup at a time, and cook, stirring constantly, for approximately 20 minutes. When done, the rice should be creamy, yet still slightly firm in the center.

REMOVE from the heat and stir in the cheese, peas, tomatoes, and basil. Season with salt and pepper. Serve.

FOR BABY: Pulse ½ cup risotto with 3 tablespoons liquid in a mini processor until the desired consistency is reached. Add more liquid if necessary.

TIDBIT: The humble pea pod is a source of iron, which moves oxygen through the body—an essential part of baby's brain development.

SUITABLE FOR FREEZING.

veggie fried rice

MAKES 4 CUPS (EIGHT ½-CUP SERVINGS)

> 2 eggs, beaten
> ½ teaspoon tamari or low-sodium soy sauce
> ½ teaspoon sesame oil
> 1 tablespoon coconut oil or olive oil
> 1 garlic clove, minced
> 1 tablespoon fresh ginger, peeled and minced
> 2 cups veggies, finely diced
> 2 cups cooked and cooled brown rice
> Salt and pepper to taste

IN a small bowl, whisk the eggs, tamari, and sesame oil with a fork.

IN a deep sauté pan, heat the oil over medium-high heat. Sauté the garlic and ginger until lightly browned, about 2 minutes. Add all the diced vegetables and cook until they are tender and sizzling, 3 to 5 minutes. Add the rice and stir until heated through, then add the eggs. Cook, stirring for a few more minutes until the eggs are cooked.

TIDBIT: Egg protein is often considered the perfect protein. It supplies all the essential amino acids, which are essential because the body cannot make them on its own. They form the building blocks for hormones, skin, tissues, and more.

SUITABLE FOR FREEZING.

kale chips

MAKES 6 SERVINGS

> 1 bunch kale
> 1 tablespoon olive oil
> Sprinkle of sea salt

PREHEAT the oven to 375°F. Line 2 baking sheets with parchment paper.

WASH and remove the stems from the kale and cut the leaves into 2-inch pieces.

DIVIDE the kale between the prepared baking sheets. Drizzle with the oil and salt, and toss to coat. Make sure there is a bit of space between the pieces of kale so they don't steam.

BAKE for 18 to 20 minutes, keeping an eye on them during the last few minutes of cooking so they don't burn.

TIP: Store kale chips in a resealable bag on the countertop, as refrigerating will soften the leaves.

TIP: Spice it up by adding a few pinches of seasoning, such as an Italian or Greek blend of spices.

TIDBIT: The beautiful leaves of the kale plant provide an earthy flavor and more nutritional value per calorie than almost any other food.

lemon caper wild salmon patties with lemon dill aioli

MAKES 10 MINI PATTIES

One of my personal favorites, I double the recipe for the whole family and take leftovers for lunches. Plus, it comes with a dip, and toddlers love to dip! Serve this with steamed broccoli and brown rice on the side.

1 pound fresh wild salmon
½ shallot, diced
1 egg
1 tablespoon fresh dill
1 tablespoon capers, drained
1 tablespoon fresh lemon juice
1 teaspoon sea salt
1 tablespoon coconut oil or olive oil

Lemon Dill Aioli
¼ cup plain Greek yogurt
¼ cup mayonnaise
1 garlic clove, minced
1 tablespoon fresh dill, chopped
Squeeze of fresh lemon
Pinch of salt

PLACE the salmon, shallot, egg, dill, capers, lemon juice, and salt in a food processor and pulse until the mixture pulls away from the sides of the bowl and creates a ball.

FORM the mixture into small patties, flattening to ensure even thickness throughout.

IN a small bowl, mix all the ingredients for the lemon dill aioli.

IN a large skillet, heat the coconut oil over medium-high heat. Brown the patties on both sides for 4 to 5 minutes per side.

SERVE the patties with the lemon dill aioli.

TIDBIT: Salmon is an incredible source of omega-3s EPA and DHA, both of which are important to healthy brain and eye development in babies.

TIDBIT: Dill is a good source of iron, magnesium, and calcium. It can be "strengthening" for the spleen, liver, and stomach organs.

SUITABLE FOR FREEZING.

teenie beanie burgers

MAKES 8 MINI PATTIES

For the longest time, my kids thought these handy little snacks were cookies—because I told them they were!

- 1 teaspoon olive oil
- ½ onion, diced
- 1 garlic clove, minced
- 1 carrot, peeled and grated
- ½ red pepper, finely diced
- ½ teaspoon cumin
- Two (15-ounce) cans chickpeas, drained and rinsed
- ½ cup fresh parsley
- ½ cup plain breadcrumbs
- ½ teaspoon salt
- 1 egg

PREHEAT the oven to 400°F. Line a baking sheet with parchment paper.

HEAT the oil in a frying pan over medium heat. Sauté the onion and garlic until soft, about 5 minutes. Add the carrots, pepper, and cumin, then sauté for another 5 minutes. Remove from the heat and cool slightly.

IN a food processor combine the onion mixture, chickpeas, parsley, breadcrumbs, salt, and egg. Pulse until the mixture pulls away from the sides of the bowl and forms a ball.

FORM the mixture into 2-inch patties; ensure the same thickness throughout for even cooking.

BAKE the patties on the prepared baking sheet for 25 minutes, flipping them halfway through to crisp on both sides.

SERVE the patties on their own, with a favorite dipping sauce, or in a mini bun or pita with your favorite toppings.

TIP: If pressed for time, panfry on the stovetop with 1 tablespoon olive oil, cooking 3 to 4 minutes per side.

TIP: If eating a burger in a bun is too cumbersome for your baby or toddler, serve the patty on its own with a spiced mayo dip or plain ketchup. Babies love to dip and feed themselves—just show them how to do it, and they will follow!

TIDBIT: Chickpeas are a good vegan source of calcium and iron.

Can be made gluten-free by substituting the breadcrumbs with gluten-free crumbs.

SUITABLE FOR FREEZING.

summer strawberry quinoa salad

MAKES 6 CUPS (TWELVE ½-CUP SERVINGS)

On a trip to the farmers' market, I filled up on the most beautifully red and ripe handpicked strawberries. With the other seasonal produce I found there, I put together a light and refreshing quinoa salad that my kids adored as much as I did. This version yields a double recipe, as I know you will love it just as much as your little one does. Keep the leftovers in the fridge for the following day's lunch.

½ cup quinoa

¼ cup jicama, peeled and diced

2 apricots, fresh or sulfate-free dried, diced

½ zucchini, diced

1 ripe avocado, peeled, pitted, and diced

1 cup strawberries, quartered

½ yellow pepper, seeded and diced

Lime Dressing

4 tablespoons extra-virgin olive oil

2 tablespoons fresh lime juice

Zest and juice of one orange

1 tablespoon fresh cilantro, chopped

2 tablespoons fresh mint, chopped

Sea salt to taste

RINSE the quinoa thoroughly and place in a medium saucepan with 1 cup water. Bring to a boil and then reduce to a simmer for 20 minutes. Fluff with a fork and remove from the heat.

IN a large bowl, combine the jicama, apricots, zucchini, avocados, strawberries, yellow peppers, and quinoa. In a separate small bowl, whisk together all the dressing ingredients. Pour the dressing over the salad, toss to combine, and refrigerate. Serve cold.

TIDBIT: NASA researchers declared quinoa the perfect snack for astronauts because it is mineral-rich and gluten-free and contains all the essential amino acids.

strawberry chocolate chia mousse

MAKES 2 CUPS (FOUR ½-CUP SERVINGS)

> 3 teaspoons unsweetened cocoa powder
> 1 tablespoon maple syrup (more or less depending on how sweet you want it)
> 2 teaspoons vanilla extract
> ½ teaspoon cinnamon
> One (14-ounce) can coconut milk
> ¼ cup water
> ¼ cup chia seeds
> ½ cup strawberries, fresh or frozen

ADD all the ingredients to a blender. Blend on high for 60 seconds, until the chia seeds are ground.

PLACE the mixture in a resealable container in the refrigerator to set. It takes 4 to 6 hours for chia to expand and develop a mousse-like texture. You can store in the fridge for up to 4 days.

TIP: Try using 4 to 6 pitted dates for added sweetness instead of syrup.

TIDBIT: Cocoa is very high in catechins, which may protect your child's skin from sun damage. Use cocoa that's at least 70 percent pure to make sure you're getting the most benefit.

mango coconut rice pudding

MAKES 4 CUPS (EIGHT ½-CUP SERVINGS)

> 1½ cups jasmine rice
> One (14-ounce) can coconut milk
> 1½ cups milk
> 2 tablespoons agave syrup
> ½ teaspoon nutmeg
> ½ teaspoon salt
> 2 ripe mangoes, peeled, seeded, and pureed

SIMMER the rice, coconut milk, milk, agave, nutmeg, and salt, uncovered, in a medium saucepan over low heat. Stir frequently until it thickens, approximately 45 minutes.

STIR in the mango puree. Serve.

TIP: Top with fresh diced mangoes, bananas, papayas, or toasted flaked coconut.

TIDBIT: Ripe mango is high in vitamin A, which helps baby's eyesight.

Make dairy-free by substituting the milk with 1 more can of coconut milk.

Keep stored in the refrigerator for up to 3 days.

sweet potato pie brownies

MAKES 16 BROWNIES

Olive oil cooking spray
1 cup whole wheat flour
½ cup unsweetened cocoa powder
1 teaspoon cinnamon
1 teaspoon baking powder
¼ teaspoon sea salt
1 cup sweet potato puree
½ cup agave nectar or maple syrup
¼ cup coconut oil, melted
3 eggs
1 teaspoon pure vanilla extract

Icing (optional)
½ cup low-fat plain cream cheese, at room temperature
3 tablespoons agave nectar or maple syrup
1 tablespoon unsweetened cocoa powder
½ teaspoon cinnamon

PREHEAT the oven to 350°F. Lightly spray an 8 x 8-inch baking pan with cooking spray.

IN a medium bowl, combine the flour, cocoa powder, cinnamon, baking powder, and salt, then set aside. In another bowl, whisk together the sweet potato puree, agave, coconut oil, eggs, and vanilla.

GRADUALLY mix the wet ingredients into the dry ingredients, until just combined. Do not overmix.

POUR the batter into the prepared pan and place it into the oven. Bake for 18 to 20 minutes, or until a toothpick inserted into the center comes out clean. Remove the pan from the oven and allow the brownies to cool to room temperature, about 30 minutes.

TO make the icing (if using), in a small bowl, combine the cream cheese, agave, cocoa powder, and cinnamon. Cover and refrigerate until needed.

LOOSEN the brownie slab and turn it out onto a cutting board or platter. Cut into 16 pieces, wrap with plastic wrap, and refrigerate overnight.

TO serve, divide the icing evenly over each brownie. Leftovers may be kept refrigerated in a resealable container for up to 2 days.

Can be made gluten-free by substituting the flour with a gluten-free blend.

SUITABLE FOR FREEZING.

chocolate coconut granola bars

MAKES 18 LITTLE BARS

These are a staple in our house and a recipe that circulates among all my friends with kids. Make a big batch and freeze individual bars for quick on-the-go snacks. I like to freeze these because it gives them a chewier texture.

> 3 cups old-fashioned rolled oats (not instant)
> 1 cup unsweetened shredded coconut
> 1 cup mini chocolate chips
> ⅓ cup whole wheat flour
> ½ cup flax meal
> 1 teaspoon cinnamon
> ½ teaspoon salt
> ¾ cup applesauce
> ½ cup honey
> ¼ cup butter or coconut oil, melted
> 1 teaspoon pure vanilla extract

PREHEAT the oven to 350°F.

LINE a 9 x 13-inch pan with parchment paper, letting the paper hang over the sides of the pan.

COMBINE the first 7 ingredients in a large bowl. Mix well. In a medium bowl whisk together the applesauce, honey, butter, and vanilla. Pour the wet ingredients over the dry ingredients and mix with a wooden spoon until the dry ingredients are completely coated.

POUR the wet granola mixture into the prepared pan and spread evenly to the edges. Use the back of a spoon or your hands to press down firmly until the granola is tightly packed.

BAKE on the middle rack of the oven for approximately 25 minutes, until the top is lightly browned and dry to the touch. Remove the pan from the oven and let cool completely.

USING the parchment paper overhang, pull out the cooled slab and transfer it to a cutting board. Using a sharp knife, cut the bars into 18 pieces (approximately 1½ x 4 inches each). Tightly wrap the individual bars in plastic wrap and store them in the fridge or freezer.

TIP: When cutting these, allow ample cooling time and avoid a sawing motion. Just press the knife straight down.

TIP: Try adding 3 tablespoons chia seeds or hemp hearts for added nutrition.

TIDBIT: Oats contain magnesium, which is not only needed for bone growth and nerve function but which also acts as a laxative for babies.

Can be made gluten-free by substituting wheat flour with a gluten-free blend.

Can be made dairy-free by using melted coconut oil instead of butter.

banana coconut oat cookies

MAKES 1½ DOZEN COOKIES

If you are wanting to create treats for your little ones that are not full of sugar or overly processed flours, look no further. Bananas keep this cookie moist, while the coconut and oats give it a chewy, macaroon-like texture.

> 2 large bananas, mashed
> ¼ cup coconut oil or canola oil
> ¼ cup honey
> ½ teaspoon pure vanilla extract
> 1 cup rolled oats
> ⅔ cup brown rice flour
> ¼ teaspoon baking soda
> ½ cup unsweetened shredded coconut
> Pinch of salt

PREHEAT the oven to 375°F. Line a baking sheet with parchment paper.

IN a medium bowl, combine the bananas, oil, honey, and vanilla.

IN a separate medium bowl, combine the oats, brown rice flour, baking soda, coconut, and salt.

ADD the banana mixture to the dry ingredients and blend until just combined. Do not overstir.

DROP batter by the heaping teaspoon onto the prepared baking sheet.

PLACE in the oven and bake for 15 minutes, or until lightly browned. Remove from the oven and place the cookies directly on a wire rack to cool.

TIP: Cookies are best refrigerated or frozen.

TIP: This recipe works nicely with maple syrup as a honey substitute, or no honey at all, if you want to make it a little less sweet. If you use sweetened coconut, then omit the honey.

TIDBIT: The potassium and sodium in oats are electrolytes that facilitate electrical activity in baby's brain, spinal cord, and muscles.

SUITABLE FOR FREEZING.

chapter 8
feed the whole family:
one meal, two ways

Let me tell you from experience: This will become your most flipped-to chapter in this book. Once you find recipes that work not just for baby, but for the whole family, huge swaths of the day become yours again.

When I first started making meals for my babies, I quickly realized that they were eating hearty, delicious, lovingly curated meals, while I was nibbling leftover puree and scrambling to put any dinner at all on the table. Instead of slaving away at all hours for a few slabs of frozen puree, I developed a bunch of recipes that could feed not only the baby, but the rest of us, as well.

This section is my selection of tasty, wholesome meals that can be pureed for young babies, pulsed for adventurous eaters, cut into bite-size pieces for your independent toddler, and savored whole (on a plate!) at the table by Mom and Dad. We're way beyond pureed pears here: Halibut with Black Bean Banana Salsa (page 201), Chicken and Sweet Potato Potpie (page 195), and Baked Sweet Potatoes with Maple Sour Cream (page 182) are some of the easy recipes that can feed you and your baby in one go. The notes within each recipe provide options on what to do, at what point in the recipe, for the various eaters in your family.

I have also adapted some of my favorite soup recipes to make them baby-friendly. It's often as simple as popping the finished recipe into a food processor or adding a few tablespoons of baby cereal to thicken it up. Either way, these recipes are easy, delicious, and so healthy for your entire family.

Despite the frustrations, the messes, and the food bills, never lose sight of the beauty of these few months (and they really are only that) while your baby is setting the cornerstones for the foundation of the person he or she will become. You are your baby's inspiration, so you must lead the way to good food and healthy eating. This is your noble moment, and your best opportunity to give them attitudes toward food that will carry them through life with health and happiness.

Food is nourishment, comfort, a cure for what ails you, and a means of protecting against ailments. It is a joy for the senses, for the soul, and for the mind, particularly when shared with your family and friends. Baby will see that from your family mealtimes, so try to make these the best times of the day. (And trust me, it'll be easier for you to relax and enjoy when you've had to make only one dinner.) So grab that mini processor, because we're going to sit the family down and share that one meal, two ways!

banana zucchini flax muffins

MAKES 24 MUFFINS

Zucchini flourishes in the summer months, and I'm always looking for ways to use it outside of salads and pasta. Here is a great recipe to use up extra zucchini and create healthy on-the-go muffins for your little one. I use bananas in cooking because their natural sweetness allows a recipe to decrease added sugars, and their moistness can stand in for oils and replace fat content. Lower sugar, lower fat, and that delicious banana flavor—how great is that?

- 2 cups light spelt flour
- ½ cup flax meal
- 1 teaspoon baking soda
- ½ teaspoon salt
- 3 medium ripe bananas
- 1½ cups zucchini, finely grated
- ½ cup maple syrup
- ¼ cup coconut oil, melted
- ⅔ cup plain or vanilla Greek yogurt
- 2 eggs
- ½ teaspoon vanilla

PREHEAT the oven to 375°F.

COMBINE the flour, flax, baking soda, and salt in a large mixing bowl.

IN a separate bowl, mash the bananas and stir in the zucchini, syrup, oil, yogurt, eggs, and vanilla.

POUR the banana mixture into the flour combo and stir to blend.

FILL the muffin tins three-quarters full and bake for 22 to 25 minutes. Let sit to cool or eat them straight out of the oven. They're delicious either way.

TIP: If you choose to make mini muffins, reduce the cooking time to 18 to 20 minutes.

TIDBIT: Eating flax seeds boosts the immune system and can help to protect your baby against infection.

Can be made gluten-free by substituting the flour with a gluten-free blend.

Can be made dairy-free by substituting the yogurt with a dairy alternative yogurt.

SUITABLE FOR FREEZING.

pumpkin coconut muffins

MAKES ABOUT 24 MUFFINS

Our whole family loves these muffins, so I keep a dozen in the freezer at all times for a quick grab-and-go snack or lunch box addition. I enjoy them most fresh out of the oven first thing in the morning. They are quick enough to make in the morning, and they fill the house with the most wonderful spiced aroma.

> 3 cups light spelt flour
> 4 teaspoons baking powder
> ½ teaspoon baking soda
> ½ teaspoon salt
> 1 teaspoon cinnamon
> 1 teaspoon ground ginger
> One (15-ounce) can pumpkin puree
> ⅔ cup maple syrup
> 1 cup coconut milk
> ½ cup coconut oil
> 2 eggs

PREHEAT the oven to 375°F. Line 2 muffin tins with paper liners.

COMBINE the dry ingredients and spices in a medium bowl. In a large bowl, whisk the pumpkin, maple syrup, coconut milk, coconut oil, and eggs. Add the dry ingredients and mix until moistened. Spoon into the prepared muffin tins.

BAKE 20 minutes. For mini muffins bake 12 minutes.

TIP: For a holiday treat, try substituting eggnog for the coconut milk and cut the maple syrup by ⅓ cup.

TIDBIT: Coconut oil and coconut milk contain a saturated fatty acid called lauric acid, which is also found in breast milk. Lauric acid has anti-inflammatory and antibacterial properties.

Can be made gluten-free by substituting equal parts gluten-free blend for the flour.

SUITABLE FOR FREEZING.

chocolate banana beet bread with chocolate yogurt topping

MAKES 1 LOAF (10 SLICES)

During harvest season for beets I was looking for something to do with a big bunch of fresh beets that did not include a goat cheese salad, so I came up with this moist piece of heaven for a treat. The topping is the most fun part for the kids, as they decide how to eat it. Do they spread it, dip it, or eat it on its own?

1 cup unbleached all-purpose flour
1 cup whole wheat flour
⅓ cup unsweetened cocoa powder
1 teaspoon baking soda
1 teaspoon baking powder
½ teaspoon salt
1 teaspoon vanilla
¼ cup canola oil
2 large eggs, whisked
3 small/medium bananas, mashed
½ cup honey or agave syrup
2 cups beets, grated
1 teaspoon butter, to grease loaf pan

Chocolate Yogurt Topping
1 cup vanilla Greek yogurt
1 teaspoon cocoa powder

PREHEAT the oven to 350°F. Grease a 9½ x 5½ x 2½-inch loaf pan.

IN a bowl, combine the first 6 ingredients.

IN a separate bowl, whisk the vanilla, oil, eggs, bananas, and honey until combined.

COMBINE the dry ingredients with the wet ingredients, then stir in the grated beets.

POUR the batter into the prepared loaf pan.

BAKE for 65 minutes, until a toothpick inserted in the center comes out clean.

COOL for 10 minutes, then remove the bread from the pan and cool completely. While the bread is cooling, make the chocolate yogurt topping by combining the yogurt and cocoa powder. Slice the bread and spread with a dollop of yogurt topping. Serve.

FOR BABY, 8 MONTHS+: Mix 3 tablespoons mashed banana and 1 tablespoon grated beet. For variety, stir in 1 tablespoon of Greek yogurt topping to the above suggestion.

TIDBIT: Cocoa is very high in catechins, which are believed to protect against heart disease and cancer and improve blood pressure and glucose metabolism.

Can be made gluten-free by substituting the flours with a gluten-free blend.

baked sweet potatoes with maple sour cream

MAKES 4 SERVINGS

4 medium sweet potatoes
1 tablespoon olive oil
Salt and pepper to taste
½ cup sour cream
4 teaspoons maple syrup

PREHEAT the oven to 425°F.

LINE a baking sheet with aluminum foil and set aside. Scrub the sweet potatoes and rub with olive oil, then place on the prepared baking sheet. Pierce each potato a few times with a fork.

BAKE in the oven until the potatoes are tender when pierced with a knife, 40 to 45 minutes. Allow to cool slightly.

SPLIT the potatoes open lengthwise and sprinkle with salt and pepper. Top each potato with a generous dollop of sour cream and a drizzle of maple syrup and serve immediately.

FOR BABY: Remove the pulp of one potato. Pulse in a mini processor or mash with a fork with 1 tablespoon of liquid and 1 tablespoon sour cream, until a chunky consistency is reached. Serve.

TIP: Don't have sour cream on hand? Try using plain Greek yogurt instead.

TIP: If your kids are feeling picky, simply serve the cooked potato with butter and a pinch of salt.

TIDBIT: Sweet potatoes are low on the glycemic index and digest slowly, which means they cause a gradual rise in blood sugar.

roasted rosemary parsnip fingers

MAKES 4 SERVINGS

- 4 to 8 parsnips, trimmed, peeled, and quartered lengthwise twice
- 3 tablespoons olive oil
- 1 teaspoon sea salt
- 1 teaspoon fresh rosemary, chopped (or 1 teaspoon dried)
- Pepper to taste

PREHEAT the oven to 450°F.

IN a large bowl, toss the parsnips with the olive oil, salt, rosemary, and pepper.

ARRANGE the seasoned parsnips on a baking sheet. Bake for 20 minutes, flipping halfway through.

FOR BABY: Either puree a couple of parsnip fingers in a mini processor with 2 to 4 tablespoons water until smooth, or cut into bite-size pieces for self-feeding.

TIDBIT: Parsnips' flavor peaks when the weather hits freezing.

PUREE IS SUITABLE FOR FREEZING.

chocolate cherry spinach smoothie

MAKES 2 CUPS (TWO 1-CUP SERVINGS)

Jill created this recipe for her family, and it has become a morning staple in their household. Her girls are old enough to make it for her—a wonderful thing to look forward to as kids age.

- ¾ cup cherries, fresh or frozen
- 1 banana
- 3 medium strawberries, fresh or frozen
- ⅓ cup blueberries, fresh or frozen
- 1 cup spinach
- ¾ cup chocolate almond milk

PLACE all the ingredients in a high-speed blender and blend until smooth. Serve.

TIP: If using frozen fruit you may need to add more liquid during blending.

TIDBIT: Cherries are rich in the stable antioxidant melatonin. Melatonin produces soothing effects on the brain and can help calm baby.

vanilla bean cashew chia pudding

MAKES 4 CUPS (EIGHT ½-CUP SERVINGS)

You may have noticed I have a few chia puddings in this book, and for very good reason: Chia is so darn good for you! This recipe is my classic go-to, and I usually have some in the fridge waiting to be topped with fresh berries and taken for a morning snack. My kids would eat it all the time if I gave them the choice!

1 cup raw cashews
4 cups filtered water
7 or 8 pitted dates
1 teaspoon cinnamon
1 vanilla bean pod, split, scraped, and seeded (or 1 teaspoon vanilla extract)
1 tablespoon coconut oil
½ cup chia seeds

SOAK the cashews in the filtered water for a minimum of 2 hours or overnight. Drain and rinse.

IN a blender, add the cashews, water, dates, cinnamon, vanilla bean seeds, and coconut oil. Blend on high for 3 minutes, until completely smooth.

IN a large bowl, whisk the cashew mixture with the chia seeds. Let stand for 10 to 15 minutes, whisking every 2 to 5 minutes to prevent the chia seeds from clumping.

PLACE the mixture in a resealable container in the refrigerator for up to 5 days.

TIP: Top with fresh berries.

TIDBIT: In addition to their healthful fats, cashews are a very good source of copper and magnesium, which are important for energy production and healthy bones.

corn on the cob with basil lemon butter

MAKES 4 COBS

4 ears of corn

4 tablespoons (½ stick) unsalted butter, at room temperature

2 tablespoons fresh basil, coarsely chopped

½ teaspoon grated lemon zest

1½ teaspoons freshly squeezed lemon juice

1 garlic clove, crushed

⅛ teaspoon salt

Pinch of pepper

BRING a large pot of water to a boil. Add the corn and cook until crisp and tender, about 3 minutes. Reserve ½ cup cooking water.

MEANWHILE, in a small bowl, stir together the butter, basil, lemon zest and juice, garlic, salt, and pepper.

SPREAD the herbed butter on the corn, and serve.

FOR BABY: Take out 1 ear of corn and slice the kernels off from top to bottom. Puree in the mini processor with 3 tablespoons reserved cooking water and 1 tablespoon butter mixture. Add more cooking water to the puree if a smoother consistency is desired.

TIP: Serve alongside grilled meat, such as steak or chicken.

TIDBIT: Corn is a great energy food, containing a healthy dose of protein and carbohydrates. It also makes a great finger food for older babies.

PUREED BABY FOOD SUITABLE FOR FREEZING.

roasted acorn squash with brown butter

MAKES 8 SERVINGS

2 acorn squash (2 to 3 pounds)
1 tablespoon olive oil
2 tablespoons maple syrup
½ teaspoon coarse salt
Pepper to taste
2 tablespoons butter

POSITION racks in the upper and lower thirds of the oven and preheat to 450°F.

HALVE the squash lengthwise and discard the seeds. Pare off some of the peel to create vertical stripes. Cut the squash crosswise into ½-inch-thick slices.

PLACE the squash on 2 baking sheets. Brush the tops lightly with olive oil and sprinkle with maple syrup, salt, and pepper. Roast, rotating the pans halfway through cooking, until tender and browned on the bottom, 18 to 20 minutes. Let the squash cool for 5 minutes, then transfer brown side up to a platter.

MEANWHILE, in a small skillet, cook the butter over medium heat until the foaming subsides and the butter browns, approximately 2 minutes. Spoon the butter over the squash.

FOR BABY: Pulse 2 slices of the peeled squash with 1 tablespoon of water or liquid of choice, until the desired consistency is reached. You can also dice peeled squash into bite-size pieces for self-feeding.

TIP: Makes a yummy side to roasted chicken or pork tenderloin.

TIDBIT: Always choose pure maple syrup. "Fake" syrup, usually labeled "breakfast" or "pancake" syrup, uses ingredients such as high-fructose corn syrup, cellulose gum, and caramel coloring to create a cheap knockoff.

PUREE SUITABLE FOR FREEZING.

asparagus pesto linguine

SERVES 6

12 ounces linguine
¼ cup pine nuts
1 pound thin asparagus, coarsely chopped
1 cup loosely packed fresh parsley, mint, and tarragon
1 garlic clove, chopped
⅓ cup Parmesan cheese, grated
½ lemon, juiced
⅓ cup olive oil
Sea salt and pepper to taste

BRING a large pot of water to a boil. Salt it, add the pasta, and cook until al dente, about 10 minutes. Drain, reserving 1 cup of the pasta cooking water.

WHILE the pasta is cooking, in a small skillet, toast the pine nuts until slightly browned.

USING a food processor, pulse the asparagus, herbs, garlic, cheese, pine nuts, and lemon juice. With the machine on, drizzle in the oil, adding more if necessary to form a creamy pesto.

IN a large bowl, combine the linguine, pesto, and ½ cup of the reserved cooking water. Toss to coat, season with sea salt and pepper, then serve.

FOR BABY: Remove 1 tablespoon of pesto and ¼ cup cooked pasta. Puree or pulse in a mini processor with 1 tablespoon pasta cooking water until a chunky texture is reached. Serve.

TIP: If extra pesto remains, freeze it in ice cube trays and use later for a grilled cheese spread, or add to cooked pasta for a quick meal.

TIDBIT: Asparagus is high in antioxidants and rich in folate, which promotes heart health and helps baby produce and maintain new cells.

Can be made gluten-free by using brown rice linguine noodles.

baked salmon with corn salad sauté and asparagus

MAKES 4 SERVINGS

Four (4-ounce) wild salmon fillets
1 fresh lemon, juiced
Salt and pepper to taste
2 cups corn kernels, fresh or frozen, thawed
½ red pepper, diced
½ medium onion, diced
1 cup cooked black beans, rinsed and drained
1 garlic clove, minced
1 tablespoon olive oil
1 bunch asparagus, trimmed
1 large tomato, chopped
1 cup cilantro, chopped

PREHEAT the oven to 350°F. Line a baking sheet with aluminum foil.

ARRANGE the salmon on the prepared baking sheet, top with half of the lemon juice, salt, and pepper, and bake for 12 minutes, using a fork to test doneness. When the center flakes easily and is opaque, the salmon is done; if not, bake another 2 to 3 minutes and check again. Note: If you plan to serve the fish to baby, exclude a portion of the fish from these seasonings.

IN a bowl, combine the corn, red pepper, onion, black beans, and garlic. Heat the olive oil in a skillet on medium-high and sauté the corn mixture for 5 minutes, stirring occasionally.

MEANWHILE, gently steam the asparagus in a skillet of shallow, boiling water for 4 minutes.

ONCE the corn mixture is sautéed, stir in the tomatoes, the remaining half of the lemon juice, and cilantro. Season with salt and pepper after baby's portion is removed. Remove from the heat.

TOP each salmon fillet with corn sauté and serve steamed asparagus on the side.

FOR BABY: In a mini processor pulse ¼ cup corn mixture, 1 tablespoon baked salmon, and 2 tablespoons milk or water until the desired consistency is reached.

TIDBIT: Salmon is a great source of omega-3 fatty acids, which are important for baby's brain and eye development.

TIDBIT: Sweet corn is a slowly digested carbohydrate that gives babies and kids long-lasting energy.

SUITABLE FOR FREEZING.

lentil marinara over spaghetti squash

MAKES 8 CUPS

A delicious option for Meatless Monday, this protein- and veggie-packed dinner is one I go back to again and again. Don't be turned off by the 45-minute bake time—once the squash is in the oven, this recipe couldn't be easier!

> 1 large spaghetti squash, halved lengthwise and seeded
> 1 tablespoon olive oil
> 2 garlic cloves, crushed
> 1 small onion, diced
> One (28-ounce) can diced tomatoes
> 1 teaspoon dried oregano
> One (28-ounce) can lentils, drained and rinsed
> 2 tablespoons fresh basil, chopped
> ¼ cup Parmesan cheese, finely grated
> Salt and pepper to taste

PREHEAT the oven to 400°F.

PLACE the squash, cut side up, in a baking dish. Pour ½ inch of water in the bottom of the dish. Bake until the squash is tender when pierced with a knife, approximately 45 minutes. Once slightly cooled, use a fork to pull the squash from the skin into spaghetti-like strips. Set aside.

HEAT the oil in a medium skillet. Sauté the garlic and onion on medium-high until soft, approximately 5 minutes. Add the tomatoes and oregano and bring to a gentle boil, then reduce the heat and simmer on low for 10 minutes. Add the lentils and fresh basil, then simmer on low for another 10 minutes.

TOP the squash with the lentil marinara and Parmesan, and season with salt and pepper.

FOR BABY: Pulse 3 tablespoons squash, 1 tablespoon lentil marinara, and 2 tablespoons water in a mini processor until the desired consistency is reached. Add more liquid if necessary. Cool and serve.

FOR PICKY EATERS: Remove a portion of the simple marinara sauce prior to adding the lentils. Serve tomato sauce over the spaghetti squash and top with Parmesan.

TIP: To make this recipe even easier, add lentils to a good store-bought tomato marinara in place of homemade sauce. Simmer together to warm and serve over cooked spaghetti squash.

TIDBIT: ¾ cup cooked lentils provides more potassium than a large banana and contains 13 grams of protein.

chicken and sweet potato potpie

MAKES 8 CUPS (SIXTEEN ½-CUP SERVINGS)

My family adores a good potpie. It warms the body as it warms the soul. This is a nutritious riff on the classic, using ingredients like sweet potato, spinach, and edamame for something a little different. You can make this ahead and freeze before baking for a convenient weeknight dinner, or freeze the leftover portions for baby's meals throughout the week.

2 tablespoons butter
1 small onion, chopped
2 stalks celery, chopped
1 large sweet potato, peeled and cut in ¼-inch cubes
¼ teaspoon each salt and pepper
⅓ cup unbleached all-purpose flour
2 cups low-sodium chicken broth
3 cups cooked chicken, diced
½ cup shelled edamame
2 tablespoons fresh sage, thinly sliced
⅛ teaspoon nutmeg
2 cups fresh spinach, chopped
½ cup evaporated milk or half-and-half

Biscuit Topping
½ cup unbleached all-purpose flour
½ cup whole wheat flour
2 teaspoons baking powder
½ teaspoon ground sage
¼ teaspoon salt
2 tablespoons butter
⅓ cup milk

PREHEAT the oven to 400°F.

IN a large saucepan, melt the butter over medium heat; cook the onion, celery, sweet potato, salt, and pepper for about 7 minutes.

STIR in the flour; cook, stirring for 1 minute. Gradually stir in the broth and bring to a boil. Reduce the heat and simmer until thickened and the sweet potato is tender, about 8 minutes.

STIR in the chicken, edamame, fresh sage, and nutmeg. Cook until the chicken is heated through, about 4 minutes. Stir in the spinach and evaporated milk.

recipe continues on next page

TO prepare the biscuit topping, combine the flours, baking powder, ground sage, and salt in a large bowl. Using a pastry blender, cut in the butter until the mixture resembles coarse crumbs. Stir in the milk. Form a ball with the dough, adding a bit more flour if the dough is too sticky. Roll out on a floured surface, until the dough is wide enough to cover the top of the casserole dish.

POUR the chicken mixture into a casserole dish and top with the rolled out dough. Prick the dough several times with a fork. Bake for 25 minutes, until the topping is golden brown. Let cool for 5 minutes before serving.

FOR BABY: Remove ½ cup potpie and pulse in a mini processor 5 to 15 times, with 3 tablespoons milk, until the desired consistency is reached. Cool and serve.

TIP: Try topping your pie with leftover mashed potatoes.

TIDBIT: Edamame is one of the few sources of complete protein derived from plants.

For gluten-free, substitute the flours with an all-purpose gluten-free blend.

For dairy-free, substitute the butter and evaporated milk with coconut oil and coconut milk.

For vegetarian, replace the chicken with 3 cups chopped, cooked vegetables.

SUITABLE FOR FREEZING.

mole chicken sloppy joes

MAKES 6 SERVINGS

1 medium onion, diced
1 garlic clove, minced
1 pound ground chicken
½ red bell pepper, diced
½ green bell pepper, diced
1 teaspoon cumin
1 teaspoon cinnamon
½ teaspoon paprika
1½ cups tomato sauce
1 cup cooked red kidney beans
2 tablespoons unsweetened cocoa powder
2 teaspoons ancho chili powder
Sea salt to taste
6 whole grain burger buns split in half

HEAT a large nonstick skillet over medium-high heat. Add the onion and garlic and cook, stirring frequently, until the onion is soft, 2 to 3 minutes. Add the chicken, red pepper, green pepper, cumin, cinnamon, and paprika. Cook, breaking up the chicken until no longer pink, about 8 minutes.

ADD the tomato sauce, beans, cocoa, and chili powder; bring the mixture to boil. Reduce the heat and simmer until thickened, about 5 minutes. Season with sea salt. Serve the sloppy joes on the whole grain burger buns.

FOR BABY: Remove ¼ cup mixture and pulse 5 to 15 times in a mini processor with 2 tablespoons liquid until the desired texture is reached. Alternatively, dice up the bun and scoop the chicken mixture onto pieces for baby to self-feed. Warning: This may be messy!

FOR PICKY EATERS: Omit disliked ingredients along the process and add at the end, after you have spooned baby's unseasoned portion onto buns.

TIDBIT: Ancho chilies have a sweet flavor and a medium heat and are known for anti-inflammatory and immune-boosting properties.

TIDBIT: The word "mole" comes from *molli*, the Aztec word for "sauce." Moles often feature a variety of chili peppers and other ingredients such as cocoa.

Can be made gluten-free by replacing the wheat buns with a gluten-free alternative.

SUITABLE FOR FREEZING.

turkey chili lasagna

MAKES 12 SLICES

2 teaspoons olive oil
1 large onion, finely chopped
1 large green pepper, finely sliced
1 pound ground turkey
3 garlic cloves, minced
1 teaspoon chili powder (optional)
¼ teaspoon cumin
Salt and pepper to taste
4 cups butternut squash (1 small squash), peeled, seeded, and cut into ¼-inch cubes
One (28-ounce) can whole plum tomatoes
½ cup low-sodium chicken broth
1 cup black beans, drained and rinsed
⅓ cup fresh cilantro, chopped
1½ cups cottage cheese
1 egg
One (16-ounce) package ready-to-cook, whole wheat lasagna noodles
1½ cups shredded mozzarella
¼ cup Parmesan cheese, grated

PREHEAT the oven to 375°F.

IN a large skillet, heat the oil on medium. Add the onion, green pepper, turkey, garlic, chili powder (if using), cumin, salt, and pepper. Break up the turkey with a wooden spoon until browned, about 6 minutes. Stir in the squash, tomatoes, broth, and beans, then bring to a boil. Reduce the heat to medium-low, cover, and simmer until thickened, about 20 minutes. Stir in the cilantro.

IN a small bowl, combine the cottage cheese and egg. Set aside.

IN a 9 x 13-inch baking dish, add enough turkey mixture to coat the bottom (avoiding squash pieces to prevent lumps). Arrange the lasagna noodles over top, followed by a third of the cottage cheese mixture, then a third of the turkey mixture. Repeat two more times. Top with mozzarella and Parmesan. Cover with foil and bake until bubbly, about 40 minutes. Uncover and continue baking for another 10 minutes, until the top is browned. Remove and cool for 5 minutes before serving.

FOR BABY: Take a small slice of the finished lasagna and pulse in a mini processor until the desired texture is reached.

TIP: This recipe is massive, and perfect for leftover lunches and baby food for the freezer. I freeze 4-ounce portions for my little ones' lunches—and I'll even freeze some for mine! For babies, puree extra smoothly and freeze in ice cube trays.

TIDBIT: The tryptophan in turkey has a wealth of health benefits, including elevating moods, regulating appetite, and aiding sleep.

Can be made gluten-free by using brown rice lasagna noodles.

To make dairy-free for baby, remove the chili mixture prior to preparing the lasagna and pulse in a mini processor.

SUITABLE FOR FREEZING.

ricotta pumpkin stuffed shells

MAKES 24 SHELLS

24 extra large pasta shells
1½ cups ricotta cheese
2½ cups pumpkin puree, divided
2 egg yolks
½ cup Parmesan cheese, grated, plus more for sprinkling
1 cup spinach, chopped
1 tablespoon fresh thyme leaves, minced
Pinch of nutmeg
1 cup tomato sauce
1 cup low-sodium vegetable stock
Salt and pepper to taste

HEAT the oven to 350°F.

BRING a large pot of water to a boil. Add a pinch of salt and drop in the shells. Cook for 10 minutes, stirring occasionally to prevent sticking. Drain and rinse with cold water. The shells should still be firm.

MIX the ricotta, 1½ cups pumpkin, egg yolks, Parmesan, spinach, thyme, and nutmeg together. Season with pepper, then set aside.

COMBINE the tomato sauce, remaining 1 cup pumpkin, and stock. Season with salt and pepper. Spoon a layer of sauce over the bottom of a 9 x13-inch baking dish. Fill the shells with a generous spoonful of pumpkin ricotta filling. Place the filled shells in the dish, pour the remaining tomato sauce mixture over the top, and sprinkle with extra grated Parmesan cheese and pepper. Cover with foil and bake for 25 to 30 minutes. Remove the foil and bake for an additional 5 minutes to brown.

FOR BABY: Pulse 1 or 2 shells with 1 tablespoon of liquid, 5 to 10 times, adding more liquid if necessary to reach the desired chunky texture. Serve.

TIP: Try using sweet potato mash instead of pumpkin.

TIP: Try adding cooked ground sausage or chicken to the ricotta filling for more protein.

TIDBIT: The deeper the color of the squash's flesh, the higher its beta-carotene, which has cancer- and heart disease–fighting properties.

SUITABLE FOR FREEZING.

halibut with black bean banana salsa

SERVES 4

1 cup black beans, rinsed well

2 large bananas, diced

½ cup red onion, chopped

2 tablespoons lime juice

½ cup cilantro, chopped

1 tablespoon olive oil

Four 3-ounce halibut fillets (¾ to 1 inch thick)

1 teaspoon sea salt

Pepper to taste

1 teaspoon chili powder

1 small jalapeño, cored, seeded, and finely chopped (optional)

IN a medium bowl, combine the black beans, bananas, red onion, lime juice, and cilantro. Season with salt and pepper.

HEAT the olive oil in a skillet on medium-high. Season the halibut with salt, pepper, and chili powder. If you plan to serve the fish to baby, exclude a portion of the fish from these seasonings.

COOK the fish until lightly browned and just opaque in the center, about 4 minutes per side.

SERVE the panfried halibut with salsa on top. Sprinkle with finely chopped jalapeño if desired.

FOR BABY: Pulse 3 tablespoons salsa and 1 tablespoon panfried halibut with 2 tablespoons water or milk in a mini processor 5 to 15 times, until the desired consistency is reached.

FOR PICKY EATERS: Make fish fingers! Slice raw halibut fillet into fingers; dip in flour, followed by a dip in one whisked egg, then dip once more in breadcrumbs (or crushed cornflakes). Repeat for each finger. Panfry until cooked through, approximately 4 minutes per side. Serve with baby's favorite dipping sauce.

TIDBIT: Black beans are rich in antioxidants—they have 10 times the amount you'd find in oranges!

PUREED BABY FOOD SUITABLE FOR FREEZING.

sweet potato ravioli with sage brown butter

MAKES 30 RAVIOLI, SERVES 4–6

I love the simple elegance of a brown butter sauce, and so do my kids. I use wonton wrappers in place of homemade pasta, making this dish a super fast work-night option.

Sweet Potato Ravioli
1 pound sweet potatoes or yams
2 tablespoons butter, at room temperature
1 tablespoon maple or agave syrup
Sea salt and pepper to taste
One (12-ounce) package wonton wrappers
1 large egg, beaten

Sage Brown Butter Sauce
¼ cup vegetable oil or coconut oil
2 large shallots, cut crosswise into thin rings
3 tablespoons butter
2 tablespoons fresh sage leaves, thinly sliced
½ teaspoon dried crushed pepper
¼ cup pine nuts, toasted (optional)

PREHEAT the oven to 400°F. Line a baking sheet with parchment paper.

CUT the sweet potatoes in half lengthwise; place cut side down on the prepared baking sheet. Roast until tender, about 30 minutes, then cool. Scoop the potato pulp out of the skins into a small bowl.

MASH the sweet potatoes with butter and syrup, and season with salt and pepper.

PLACE the wonton wrappers on a work surface. Using a pastry brush, paint the edges of a wrapper with beaten egg. Place ½ tablespoon sweet potato filling in the center of each wonton. Fold each wrapper diagonally over the filling, forming a triangle. Seal the edges and transfer to a baking sheet. Let stand while making the sauce.

LINE a plate with paper towels. Heat the oil in a small skillet over medium-high heat. Working in 2 batches, fry the shallots until crisp and dark brown, about 2 minutes. Using a slotted spoon, transfer the shallots to the paper towel–lined plate to drain.

COOK the butter in a large frying pan on medium heat until it begins to brown, about 3 minutes. Remove from the heat. Add the sage leaves, which will crisp up in the hot butter.

MEANWHILE, cook the wonton ravioli in a large pot of boiling salted water until tender, about 3 minutes. Drain well. Add the ravioli to the pan with the butter sauce; toss to coat.

PLATE the wonton ravioli, drizzle with the remaining sauce, and top with shallots, crushed red peppers, and pine nuts (if using). Serve immediately.

FOR BABY: In a mini processor, pulse 2 ravioli with a drizzle of brown butter. Add liquid in 1-tablespoon increments if necessary, until the desired consistency is reached.

TIDBIT: Sage contains important anti-inflammatory properties and has been used to alleviate digestive issues.

SUITABLE FOR FREEZING.

turkey parmesan strata

MAKES 6 SERVINGS

Cooking spray
3 slices whole grain bread, cut into ½-inch cubes
1 tablespoon olive oil
¼ pound ground turkey
1 small onion, finely diced
¼ teaspoon dried basil
¼ teaspoon dried parsley
¼ teaspoon sea salt
¾ cup milk
3 large eggs
2 tablespoons fresh parsley, finely chopped, plus more for sprinkling
¼ cup Parmesan cheese, grated and divided
1 large tomato, cut crosswise into 6 slices
Salt and pepper to taste

PREHEAT the oven to 375°F.

LIGHTLY mist a 6-cup casserole dish with cooking spray. Evenly line with bread cubes.

HEAT the oil in a nonstick skillet over medium heat. Add the turkey, onion, and spices and cook, breaking up the turkey and cooking through for approximately 5 minutes.

IN a small bowl, combine the milk, eggs, parsley, and half of the Parmesan. Pour the liquid over the bread cubes in the casserole dish and spoon the turkey evenly over top. Finish with a layer of tomatoes, using the back of a spatula or spoon to press them into the egg mixture until moistened. Sprinkle with the remaining Parmesan and bake until puffed and golden brown on top, approximately 40 minutes. Season with fresh parsley, salt, and pepper.

FOR BABY: Remove ½ cup of strata and pulse 5 to 15 times in a mini processor with 3 tablespoons of water or milk, until the desired consistency is reached.

TIDBIT: Eggs contain vitamins A, D, E, and B_{12}, which aid in the healthy development of baby's vision, bones, and teeth.

Can be made gluten-free by using gluten-free bread.

turkey pesto meatballs and spaghetti

MAKES 4 SERVINGS

Pesto
3 tablespoons olive oil
2 large handfuls fresh basil
1 tablespoon pine nuts, toasted
1 tablespoon lemon juice
1 tablespoon Parmesan cheese, grated
Pinch of sea salt

Turkey Meatballs and Spaghetti
1 pound ground turkey
1½ cups breadcrumbs
1 egg
4 cups tomato sauce, divided
1 pound whole wheat spaghetti
2 tablespoons Parmesan cheese, grated

IN a food processor, combine all the pesto ingredients, blending until it resembles a paste.

MIX the turkey, breadcrumbs, ¼ cup pesto, and egg in a medium bowl. Using moistened hands, form the mixture into bite-size meatballs.

SPREAD 2 cups tomato sauce over the bottom of a heavy medium skillet.

PLACE the meatballs in a single layer in the sauce. Spoon the remaining sauce on top and bring to

a simmer. Cover, reduce the heat to medium-low, and simmer until the meatballs are cooked through, stirring occasionally, about 20 minutes.

MEANWHILE, cook the pasta in a large pot of boiling salted water until just tender. Drain the pasta.

TOP the pasta with the meatballs, sauce, and Parmesan cheese.

FOR BABY: Combine 1 cooked meatball; ¼ cup pasta; 4 tablespoons water, low-sodium chicken stock, or milk; and 2 tablespoons tomato sauce from the skillet in a mini processor. Pulse until the desired consistency is reached. Alternatively, dice the meatball and pasta into bite-size pieces for self-feeding.

TIDBIT: Basil has long been used as a calming aid for indigestion.

Can be made gluten-free by substituting brown rice pasta for the whole wheat spaghetti.

SUITABLE FOR FREEZING.

butternut squash apple coconut soup

MAKES 6 SERVINGS

2 tablespoons olive oil
1 large yellow onion, chopped
1 large butternut squash, peeled, seeded, and cut into 2-inch pieces
4 large apples, peeled, cored, and quartered
4 cups vegetable stock, divided
One (14-ounce) can coconut milk
½ teaspoon nutmeg
Sea salt and pepper to taste

IN a large saucepan, heat the oil over medium-high heat. Sauté the onion until translucent, about 5 minutes. Add the squash, apples, 2 cups stock, coconut milk, and nutmeg. Cover, bring to a boil, then reduce the heat and simmer for 20 minutes, or until the squash is soft.

FOR BABY: At this point, remove ½ cup squash and apple pieces, draining liquid from the cup. Puree with 3 tablespoons cooking liquid in a mini processor until smooth. Add more cooking liquid for a thinner consistency.

FOR the rest of the family, add the remaining 2 cups vegetable stock and puree with a handheld blender until smooth and creamy. Heat through. Remove from the heat, then season with salt and pepper. Serve.

TIP: Stir in 1 tablespoon Greek yogurt and a pinch of finely chopped cilantro for an extra kick.

TIP: As a time-saver, use pre-diced frozen butternut squash.

TIDBIT: Butternut squash has more vitamin A than a pumpkin, and 1 cup contains only 63 calories.

SUITABLE FOR FREEZING.

cream of asparagus soup

MAKES 6 CUPS

2 bunches asparagus

2 tablespoons olive oil

2 garlic cloves, minced

3 leeks, white parts only, chopped

½ cup rolled oats

3 cups milk

½ teaspoon dried dill

Juice of ½ lemon

Sea salt and pepper to taste

Greek yogurt and shaved Parmesan (optional)

PREP the asparagus by snapping off the tough ends at their natural breaking point, and discard. Wash the remaining stalk, chop into 2-inch pieces, and set aside.

IN a large pot, heat the oil over medium heat. Sauté the garlic and leeks until soft, 2 to 3 minutes. Add the asparagus, oats, milk, dill, and enough water to just cover the asparagus. Bring to a gentle boil, reduce the heat, cover, and simmer until the asparagus is soft, about 10 minutes. Remove from the heat, add lemon juice, season with salt and pepper to taste, and allow to cool slightly.

PUREE the soup using a blender, food processor, or handheld blender until smooth.

TOP with Greek yogurt or shaved Parmesan if desired.

FOR BABY: Remove ½ cup soup and stir in 1 tablespoon rice or oatmeal baby cereal to create a thicker consistency.

TIP: Serve with grilled cheese croutons or a dollop of Greek yogurt.

TIDBIT: Did you know that asparagus can take the pain out of a bee sting? Just crush it up and apply to the area around the sting.

Can be made dairy-free by substituting unsweetened almond or coconut milk for the milk.

SUITABLE FOR FREEZING.

broccoli cheddar soup

MAKES 6 CUPS

2 tablespoons olive oil
1 large onion, chopped
2 garlic cloves, crushed
2 tablespoons whole wheat flour
2 pounds broccoli, stems and florets separated
and chopped into pieces
4 cups chicken stock
2 cups extra sharp cheddar, grated
1 cup evaporated skim milk
Coarse salt and pepper to taste

IN a large saucepan, heat the oil over medium-high heat. Sauté the onion and garlic for about 5 minutes, until soft, then add the flour and stir to coat well.

ADD the broccoli and chicken stock, then bring to a simmer and cover; cook for about 20 minutes, or until the broccoli is very tender.

USING a handheld immersion blender, puree the soup right in the pot (or transfer some of it to a blender or food processor to process until smooth), leaving some larger chunks if you like.

ADD the cheese and milk and heat through, stirring just until the cheese melts. Season with salt and pepper, and then serve.

TIP: To add more texture for baby, stir in some cooked quinoa or brown rice.

TIDBIT: Want something high in vitamin C, but don't feel like eating fruit? One cup of chopped broccoli has the same amount as an orange.

Can be made gluten-free by substituting the flour with a gluten-free blend.

SUITABLE FOR FREEZING.

coconut, chickpea, and lentil stew

MAKES 6 CUPS

One of my favorite stews. Between the ginger, curry, cinnamon, and coconut milk, baby's palate will be sure to develop a love of great taste. The chickpeas and lentils make this a wonderful vegetarian dish, as high in protein as it is in flavor.

1 tablespoon olive oil
1 onion, chopped
1 red pepper, finely diced
1 teaspoon fresh ginger, peeled and minced
2 garlic cloves, minced
4 teaspoons mild yellow curry powder
½ teaspoon cinnamon
2 tablespoons tomato paste
4 cups low-sodium vegetable stock
One (14-ounce) can coconut milk
2 cups red lentils
One (16-ounce) can chickpeas, drained and rinsed
Squeeze of fresh lime

HEAT the olive oil in a medium saucepan over medium-high heat. Add the onion and red pepper; cook until it softens, about 5 minutes. Add the ginger, garlic, curry, cinnamon, and tomato paste, cooking until fragrant, about 2 minutes. Add the broth, coconut milk, lentils, and chickpeas. Cook uncovered for 20 to 25 minutes. Remove from the heat and squeeze in the fresh lime juice.

USING an immersion or standard blender or a food processor, pulse until the desired texture is achieved. Serve.

TIP: For adults, season with salt, pepper, and a hint of sriracha. If the stew is too thin for baby, try stirring in some baby cereal or quinoa flakes to thicken it.

TIDBIT: Both red lentils and chickpeas are a great source of vegetarian iron and protein.

TIDBIT: The ginger in this recipe helps counteract any gas-causing effects of eating chickpeas.

SUITABLE FOR FREEZING.

chicken vegetable minestrone

MAKES 6 CUPS

2 tablespoons olive oil

2 garlic cloves, minced

1 medium onion, diced

2 carrots, peeled and sliced

1 cup mushrooms, peeled and sliced

1 small sweet potato, peeled and diced

1 small zucchini, quartered and sliced

1 cup chickpeas, drained and rinsed

5½ cups low-sodium chicken or vegetable stock

9 ounces boneless, skinless chicken breast, diced

1 cup broccoli, chopped

⅓ cup small pasta

2 tablespoons fresh parsley, chopped

IN a large nonstick saucepan, heat the oil and sauté the garlic, onions, and carrots until tender, approximately 7 minutes. Add the mushrooms and sauté an additional 4 minutes.

ADD the sweet potatoes, zucchini, chickpeas, and broth. Cover and simmer on low for 12 minutes, until the sweet potatoes are tender.

ADD the chicken, broccoli, and pasta. Simmer until the chicken is cooked, approximately 12 minutes.

GARNISH with parsley and serve.

FOR BABY: Remove ½ cup of soup and pulse in a mini processor until a chunky consistency is reached. Cool and serve.

TIDBIT: Mushrooms are the only fruit or vegetable that contains vitamin D. Like humans, mushrooms produce vitamin D when in sunlight. Vitamin D is essential to bone formation and may aid in preventing autoimmune disease.

SUITABLE FOR FREEZING.

italian-style hamburger soup

MAKES 6 CUPS

When I was a kid, we ate hamburger soup all the time. My dad made it, usually chock-full of jalapeño or habanero peppers, which never failed to burn my lips. For this recipe, I've left out the hot stuff and kept all the rich Italian-style flavors. My kids loved the simple version of this soup as babies and now eat it warmed in their thermoses for lunch. Make a double batch to freeze leftovers.

1 tablespoon olive oil
1 large onion, finely diced
4 garlic cloves, minced
2 medium carrots, peeled and thinly sliced
1 cup celery, thinly sliced
1 cup zucchini, thinly sliced
1 pound ground beef
1½ teaspoons Italian herb seasoning
One (28-ounce) can diced tomatoes
4 cups low-sodium chicken broth
One (5½-ounce) can tomato paste
1 cup fresh spinach, chopped
¼ cup fresh parsley, chopped
½ cup whole wheat spaghetti, broken
Salt and pepper to taste

IN a large saucepan, heat the olive oil over medium heat. Sauté the onion and garlic for 2 minutes. Add the carrots, celery, zucchini, ground beef, and Italian seasoning. Cook until the meat is cooked through, approximately 10 minutes.

ADD the diced tomatoes, chicken broth, and tomato paste. Bring to a boil, then reduce the heat to a simmer for 15 minutes.

ADD the spinach, parsley, and spaghetti. Simmer for 10 minutes. Season with salt and pepper.

FOR BABY: Remove ½ to 1 cup of soup and puree or pulse in a mini processor until the desired consistency is reached. Cool and serve.

TIDBIT: Cooking tomatoes and meat in an iron pot boosts the iron content of food even more, as the acidity of the tomatoes draws the iron from the pot and into the food.

SUITABLE FOR FREEZING.

veggie, beef, and barley stew

MAKES 6 TO 8 SERVINGS

One of Baby Gourmet's top-selling products at the farmers' market, this is a hearty meal the whole family will love!

4 ounces stewing beef, diced into ¼-inch cubes
Salt and pepper to taste
2 tablespoons olive oil, divided
1 large onion, diced
2 garlic cloves, minced
4 celery stalks, sliced
4 carrots, peeled and sliced
2 cups mushrooms, peeled and sliced
6 cups beef stock
½ cup pearl barley
4 small potatoes, diced into ½-inch cubes (or 18 minis quartered)
2 tablespoons Montreal Steak Seasoning
2 tablespoons fresh parsley, chopped

PAT the beef dry with a paper towel and season with salt and pepper.

IN a large saucepan, heat 1 tablespoon oil over medium-high heat. Just brown the beef on all sides, 4 to 5 minutes total. Remove the browned beef and set aside.

IN the same pan, add the remaining 1 tablespoon oil and sauté the onion and garlic until lightly browned, about 3 minutes.

ADD the celery, carrots, and mushrooms. Sauté another 10 minutes, until cooked through.

ADD the beef stock, barley, potatoes, Montreal Steak Seasoning, and browned beef. Bring to a boil, then reduce the heat and simmer on low for 50 minutes.

STIR in fresh parsley before serving.

FOR BABY: Remove ½ cup stew and pulse in a mini processor until a chunky consistency is reached. Cool and serve.

TIP: You can use chicken stock in place of beef stock if you prefer.

TIP: Serve with homemade cheddar biscuits or toasted garlic focaccia bread on the side.

TIDBIT: Parsley is a powerful herb. It's a good source of calcium and has more vitamin C than citrus fruits, so if your baby can't eat citrus fruits, adding parsley to their food is a great alternative. It helps the body's defense mechanisms, which can keep harmful bacteria at bay.

SUITABLE FOR FREEZING.

chicken tortilla chili

MAKES 6 SERVINGS

1 tablespoon olive oil

2 garlic cloves, minced

½ medium onion, diced

¼ teaspoon chili powder

1 pound ground chicken

Two (14½-ounce) cans diced tomatoes in juice

One (15-ounce) can black beans, drained and rinsed

One (14½-ounce) can reduced-sodium chicken broth

One (10-ounce) package frozen corn kernels

Sea salt and pepper to taste

1 cup crushed tortilla chips, plus more for serving (optional)

1 tablespoon fresh lime juice

1 ripe avocado, peeled, pitted, and diced

2 tablespoons cilantro, chopped

½ cup Monterey Jack cheese (or any other hard cheese on hand), grated

IN a large saucepan, heat the oil over medium heat. Cook the garlic, onion, and chili powder until fragrant, about 2 minutes. Add the ground chicken and sauté until cooked, 5 to 7 minutes. Add the tomatoes (with juice), beans, broth, corn, and 1 cup water; season with salt and pepper. Bring the soup to a boil, then reduce to a simmer for 20 minutes.

ADD the tortilla chips; cook until softened, about 2 minutes. Remove from the heat and stir in the lime juice, avocado, and cilantro. Season with salt and pepper. Sprinkle with cheese and additional tortilla chips (if using) before serving.

TIDBIT: Cilantro not only brings great flavors to a recipe, but it also acts as a natural healing agent and strong antioxidant.

TIDBIT: Did you know an avocado is actually a fruit?

TIDBIT: It's not just about health: Chicken that's organically raised tends to be more tender and have more complex flavors.

Can be made dairy-free by omitting the cheese topping.

SUITABLE FOR FREEZING.

acknowledgments

This book has been a work in progress ever since I started making my daughter's baby food ten years ago. Over the years I have had numerous requests for recipes, tips, and techniques around feeding baby, and it was only a matter of time before I was freed up to focus on this passion project. A big thanks goes out to all our customers (babies and kids), moms, dads, and caregivers whose support of Baby Gourmet allows us to do what we love to do by creating delicious, healthy recipes and encouraging a love for good food from the first bite.

I would also like to send out many thanks to the incredible team behind our company, which is often referred to as "the little engine that could." You know who you are, and if I don't tell you enough, we couldn't have achieved our heights without you.

More love to send out to the incredible team who contributed to, designed, and photographed this beautiful book: Marnie Burkhart at Jazhart Studios Inc., Jen House from First Step Nutrition, and Karen, Crystal, Lisa, and Sarah from Evans Hunt. You are all so talented and patient!

Finally, to the most supportive and inspiring family I could ever ask for, thank you from the bottom of my heart. Thank you, Mom, for all your creative homemade meals, the backyard garden you painstakingly cultivated for us kids, and for passing on your love of food. Jill, the yin to my yang, for taking this leap of faith and believing in my vision. I couldn't and wouldn't have wanted to embark on this roller coaster without you. Cliff, for your continued love, encouragement, and creativity. Thank you!

Last but not least, thank you to all my recipe testers over the years: Finley, Eamon, Tatum, Sage, Brynn, Declan, Casey, Abby, and Lincoln. Your inspiration and criticism made this book all it could be!

about the author

JENNIFER CARLSON is the visionary, innovator, and, along with cofounding sister, Jill Vos, recipe developer of multimillion-dollar Baby Gourmet Foods Inc., an organic baby food company specializing in nutritious and delicious packaged food for babies and toddlers. She launched the Baby Gourmet brand at a local farmers' market in 2006 and has since built a company with products distributed in major retailers across North America. She and her team secured national Canadian retail distribution in February 2011 in retailers such as Walmart, Loblaws, Safeway, and Sobeys. Baby Gourmet is now Canada's leading brand of organic baby food and is available in over 90 percent of stores where baby food is sold in Canada. The kids' line of healthy snacking products, Slammers, are sold nationwide in the United States in over 4400 stores, including Target, Safeway, Publix, HEB, Kroger, and Walmart. Baby Gourmet is currently in talks to expand the baby food line nationwide in the United States.

Jen is the mother of two well-fed children, a visionary, innovator, and an inspirational and motivating speaker to women, entrepreneurs, and busy moms. Jen has been recognized for her leadership, innovation, and entrepreneurial spirit over the years, receiving the 2011 Ernst & Young Emerging Entrepreneur of the Year (Prairies region) and ranking #7 on PROFIT/Chatelaine W100, top Canadian women entrepreneurs. The Baby Gourmet brand reaches millions of moms each month through coverage on TV (such as Food Network's *Food Factory*) and in popular blogs (such as BabyCenter), in magazines including *Women's Day*, and on websites including *Huffington Post* and People.com.

JENNIFER HOUSE is a registered dietitian, mom of three, and owner of First Step Nutrition, a company specializing in complete family nutrition. She brings extensive experience in the areas of nutrition for pregnant and postpartum moms, babies, and young children. She is passionate about nourishing a growing family with confidence.

notes

CHAPTER ONE

1. "Infant Feeding," *Health Canada*, last modified July 6, 2015, http://www.hc-sc.gc.ca/fn-an/nutrition/infant-nourisson/index-eng.php.

2. Edmond S. Chan and Carl Cummings, "Dietary Exposures and Allergy Prevention in High-Risk Infants," *Canadian Paediatric Society*, posted on December 2, 2013, http://www.cps.ca/documents/position/dietary-exposures-and-allergy-prevention-in-high-risk-infants.

3. "LEAP Study Results," *Immune Tolerance Network*, accessed on March 16, 2016, http://www.leapstudy.co.uk/.

4. M. Morzel, O. Palicki, C. Chabanet, G. Lucchi, P. Ducoroy, C. Chambon, and S. Nicklaus, "Saliva Electrophoretic Protein Profiles in Infants: Changes with Age and Impact of Teeth Eruption and Diet Transition," *Archive of Oral Biology* 56, no. 7 (2011): 634–42, doi: 10.1016/j.archoralbio.2010.12.015.

5. G. P. Sevenhuysen, C. Holodinsky, and C. Dawes, "Development of Salivary Alpha-Amylase in Infants from Birth to 5 Months," *The American Journal of Clinical Nutrition* 39, no. 4 (1984): 584–8, http://www.ncbi.nlm.nih.gov/pubmed/6608871.

6. Balba Kurins Gillard, Janet A. Simbala, and Lee Goodglick, "Reference Intervals for Amylase Isoenzymes in Serum and Plasma of Infants and Children," *Clinical Chemistry* 29, no. 6 (1983): 1119–1123, http://www.ncbi.nlm.nih.gov/pubmed/6189641. M. D. O'Donnell and N. J. Miller, "Plasma Pancreatic and Salivary-Type Amylase and Immunoreactive Trypsin Concentrations: Variations with Age and Reference Ranges for Children," *Clinica Chimica Acta: International Journal of Clinical Chemistry* 104, no. 3 (1980): 265–73, doi: 10.1016/0009-8981(80)90384–8.

7. M. Mobassaleh, R. K. Montgomery, J. A. Biller, and R. J. Grand, "Development of Carbohydrate Absorption in the Fetus and Neonate," *Pediatrics* 75, no. 1 (1985): 160–6, http://www.ncbi.nlm.nih.gov/pubmed/2578223.

8. P. C. Lee, S. Werlin, B. Trost, and M. Struve, "Glucoamylase Activity in Infants and Children: Normal Values and Relationship to Symptoms and Histological Findings," *Journal of Pediatric Gastroenterology and Nutrition* 39, no. 2 (2004): 161–5, doi: 10.1097/00005176-200408000-00007.

9. G. Zoppi, G. Andreotti, F. Pajno-Ferrara, D. M. Njai, and D. Gaburro, "Exocrine Pancreas Function in Premature and Full Term Neonates," *Pediatric Research* 6, no. 12 (1972): 880–6, doi: 10.1203/00006450-197212000-00005.

10. T. Lindberg and G. Skude, "Amylase in Human Milk," *Pediatrics* 70, no. 2 (1982): 235–8, http://www.ncbi.nlm.nih.gov/pubmed/6179037.

11. L. A. Heitlinger, P. C. Lee, W. P. Dillon, and E. Lebenthal, "Mammary Amylase: A Possible Alternate Pathway of Carbohydrate Digestion in Infancy," *Pediatric Research* 17, no. 1 (1983): 15–18, http://www.ncbi.nlm.nih.gov/pubmed/6188091.

12. A. Stephen, et al., "The role and requirements of digestible dietary carbohydrates in infants and toddlers," *European Journal of Clinical Nutrition* 66, no. 7 (2012): 765–79, doi: 10.1038/ejcn.2012.27.

13. Anna Chmielewska, Hania Szajewska, and Raanan Shamir, "Celiac disease—prevention strategies through early infant nutrition," *World Review of Nutrition and Dietetics* 108, (2013): 91–97, doi: 10.1159/000351491.

14. Bill Hendrick, "Study Shows Greater Risk of Allergies for Kids and Adolescents Who Don't Get Enough Vitamin D," MedicineNet.com, posted on February 25, 2011, http://www.medicinenet.com/script/main/art.asp?articlekey=126415.

15. "Nutrition for Healthy Term Infants: Recommendations from Six to 24 Months," *Health Canada,* last modified on January 19, 2015, http://www.hc-sc.gc.ca/fn-an/nutrition/infant-nourisson/recom/recom-6-24-months-6-24-mois-eng.php#a5.

16. "Ellyn Satter's Division of Responsibility in Feeding," *Ellyn Satter Institute,* accessed November 9, 2015, http://www.ellynsatterinstitute.org.

17. For more info on "dirty" and "clean" produce with regards to pesticides, see "EWG's 2015 Shopper's Guide to Pesticides in Produce," Environmental Working Group, accessed on November 9, 2015, http://www.foodnews.org/.

CHAPTER TWO

1. C.f. "Non-GMO Project," accessed on November 9, 2015, http://www.nongmoproject.org.

2. C.f. The Canadian Food Inspection Agency, "Labelling Requirements for Meat and Poultry Products," http://www.inspection.gc.ca/food/labelling/food-labelling-for-industry/meat-and-poultry-products/eng/1393979114983/1393979162475.

3. This is a good explanation on organic meat in Canada, quoted from "What Is Organic Meat?," The Healthy Butcher, accessed on November 9, 2015, http://www.thehealthybutcher.com/organics.html.

4. "Guidelines on Natural, Naturally Raised, Feed, Antibiotic and Hormone Claims," Canadian Food Inspection Agency, last modified on May 26, 2016, https://email15.secureserver.net/webmail.php?login=1#_msocom_1.

5. "Addendum A: EPA and DHA Content of Fish Species," USDA, accessed on November 9, 2015, http://www.health.gov/dietaryguidelines/dga2005/report/html/table_g2_adda2.htm.

6. For more information on sustainable seafood, check out www.seachoice.org.

7. Check out http://www.localharvest.org to find the farmers' markets near you.

8. For detailed seasonal food guides, check out www.eatwellguide.org or www.simplesteps.org. For a country-specific guide see www.sustainabletable.org for U.S. residents and http://localfoods.about.com/od/CanadianProduceGuides/ for Canadian residents. For more on eating locally in Canada see http://www.farmersmarketsincanada.com.

index

Printed in the United States
By Bookmasters